NARROW GAUGE RAILWAYS OF SPAIN

Volume 1
Catalunya to the Sierra Nevada

D. Trevor Rowe

Plateway Press, PO Box 973, Brighton, BN2 2TG
ISBN   1 871980 24 0

© D. Trevor Rowe/ Plateway Press 1995

All rights reserved. No part of this publication may be reproduced, stored in a retrieval system, or transmitted, in any form or by any means, electronic, mechanical, photocopying, recording or otherwise, without the prior written permission of the Publisher.

Printed in Great Britain by Postprint, Taverner House, Harling Road, East Harling, Norfolk.

ISBN 1 871980 24 0

Cover artwork by John Holroyd

Typesetting by   Ian Miller / Intersoft Multimedia (English text)
                      Ted Relton / Rapid Transit Publications (Spanish text)

Book design by Keith Taylorson

Maps by David H. Smith

Front cover illustration: a mixed train on the 75 cm gauge San Feliu - Gerona railway pauses at Llagostera.
(collection - Keith Taylorson)

Back cover illustration: a rare colour view of a train ascending the Montserrat rack railway, which closed in 1957. *(Author's collection)*

Frontispiece: 0-6-0WT No 9 halts in the town square of Castellon de la Plana before continuing its journey to Grao de Castellon on 5 April 1961. *(Author)*

INTRODUCTION

It is now over 30 years since publication of *'Steam on the Sierra'* by Peter Allen and Robert Wheeler. This book, which has become a much sought after classic, helped to stimulate the interest of British railway enthusiasts in Spain long before package holidays and mass tourism brought about the rush to the 'costas'. This rush, alas, came just too late to save such gems as the San Feliu-Gerona railway, which today would no doubt rate as a first class tourist attraction and be subsidised by the regional authorities. It is ironic that in the past few years a number of books have been published in Spain on the narrow gauge there, many of which are partially illustrated by British enthusiasts, who were virtually the only ones to show interest before the railways concerned closed or were modernised. The books are almost all 'in depth' studies of individual lines, and virtually nothing comprehensive on the country as a whole has appeared to date, translations of British works, including *'Steam on the Sierra'*, excepted.

The Spanish narrow gauge offered fantastic variety, probably greater than any other European country in the post-war years. From an electrified main line of metre gauge with locomotive hauled expresses incorporating Pullman cars, one could range through long, rambling routes with maybe only a daily 'correo' stopping at all stations and in at least one instance incorporating a lunch break reminiscent of Swindon in broad gauge days! Busy suburban systems, usually only partially electrified, served cities such as Valencia, Bilbao and Barcelona, while steam trains could be found bustling through the streets of towns such as Castellon de la Plana, or alongside country roads in Castile or Cantabria. In Madrid one could change, cross platform if such a thing had existed, from a city tram to a one coach steam train for the final stage of the journey to Colmenar Viejo, or set out from an underground terminus beneath a central square of Barcelona behind electric traction, to end up in the mountains at the remote town of Guardiola, from whence it was possible to continue even further on a lesser gauge mixed train owned and operated by a cement company! Industrial lines in the north of Spain were legion, some of unusual gauges, some having built their own motive power, and quite a few with workmen's trains on which it was possible to cadge a ride! At the other end of the scale, long industrial lines linked Utrillas with Zaragoza, and the Ojos Negros mines with a steelworks at Sagunto, while similar railways in the south, such as Río Tinto and Tharsis, are almost household names to the enthusiast.

With *'Steam on the Sierra'* out of print, and rare second-hand copies commanding high prices, it is time to take another look at the Spanish narrow gauge as it was in the 1950s and 1960s, and this publication sets out to cover both steam and electric lines of gauges less than the European standard, thus excluding certain lines in Barcelona and the early history of the Langreo line in Northern Spain. The island of Mallorca and Río Tinto are also excluded as separate publications have recently been devoted to them. City tramways are also excluded, although towns such as Granada had interurban lines which were quite scenic.

Most of the railways depicted in this book have gone, sometimes without trace, but the Spanish narrow gauge is by no means dead, as is virtually the case in France, and in Britain apart from tourist lines. The narrow gauge that remains in Spain is all 'working' railway, some 2000km of it, modernised and in most cases operated or subsidised by the state or regional authorities, and usually with a bright future. Nowadays one can travel without a break on the metre gauge from Hendaye in France to El Ferrol, more than 800km over the tracks of (nowadays) just two organisations, using both electric and diesel traction. The long La Robla Railway has lost its through passenger service but remains (though by no means secure) as do some of the industrial lines in the area. Also the Catalanes system at Barcelona, now much truncated, and the Valencia suburban railways, now much improved with two formerly separate systems physically linked at last. Electrified mountain lines such as Ribas-Núria (part-rack) and Cercedilla-Los Cotos (adhesion) survive and flourish, and in 1990 there was even talk of reconstructing the Montserrat Rack Railway to cope with the volume of tourists visiting the monastery. The modern scene is not overlooked, and a few illustrations interspersed with the 'nostalgic' ones, will help to convince modern traction enthusiasts that Spain still has much to offer.

The majority of photographs in this book have not been published before in the UK, although there are exceptions where the subject is of particular interest and other illustrations have not been available, while others have been used in Spanish publications. The bibliography (included in Part 2) lists sources (books or magazine articles) where further information on certain railways or industrial concerns can be found. In some, but not all, cases, these may have served as sources for this work, which tries to steer the difficult course of being more than just a photo-album but less than an authoritative and detailed history.

A LITTLE BACKGROUND HISTORICAL INFORMATION will be of use to readers and help them appreciate the changes which have taken place in Spain during the last 25 years or so. With one or two exceptions, the earliest photographs in this book date back to the 1950s, when Spain was a very poor country and tourism totally undeveloped and uncommercialised. In the early 1950s a visa was needed to enter the country and rail travel had changed little since before the Civil War (1936-39). The broad gauge RENFE had been the National system since 1941, but on the narrow gauge most companies were independent, although the ESTADO (State) organisation had been set up as early as 1926 to keep open failed lines which it was not deemed in the public interest to allow to close. Thus, very few closures indeed of narrow gauge public railways had taken place by the 1950s, although one or two had been broad-gauged and incorporated into the RENFE, an example being Silla-Cullera (Valencia) in 1935. Tudela-Tarazona followed in 1952 and an early closure was Mollerusa-Balaguer in 1952. There were a few more closures in the 1950s, Gerona-Palamós and both electric and steam lines around Pamplona being examples, but in general as lines became uneconomic the ESTADO took over, and by the end of the decade, introduced diesel locomotives and railcars in an effort to cut costs and improve services.

Figures published in 1965 claimed some 4300km of narrow gauge (against 5300 some years earlier), with a total of 607 locomotives, 450 of which were steam (railcars/electric units excluded). This was the year in which the ESTADO (Explotación de Ferrocarriles por el Estado) became the FEVE (Ferrocarriles del Estado de Vía Estrecha) and a growing number of lines were being taken over as the original companies failed. By 1969 many had been closed, as with limited resources FEVE could only concentrate on the more profitable systems, achieving, for example, the completion of the northern coastline link between El Ferrol and Gijón in 1972. With the arrival of democratic government soon after, this power devolved to regional authorities and suburban systems serving cities such as Valencia and Barcelona became the responsibility of the local Generalitat. Way back in 1942 a plan was published suggesting linking almost all the Spanish metre gauge by the construction of a few relatively short sections, but this over ambitious scheme, like many others, never came to pass.

This survey of the Spanish narrow gauge, past and present, starts out in Catalonia, and roughly follows the Mediteranean coastline right round to the southern Portuguese border, turning inland to cross central southern Spain, part one terminating at Granada. Part two will start with Madrid, rather isolated as far as narrow gauge is concerned, returning from the capital to the French frontier via a few isolated lines in the north before embarking on the long northern coastal trip to El Ferrol, a journey which can be undertaken today, but was not possible throughout until 1972. As well as public railways, many industrial concerns will receive mention, although it would be impossible to cover them all in a region such as this, where the narrow gauge is the 'main line' and the broad gauge reaches the coast only at intervals.

D. Trevor Rowe
Horley, Surrey
December 1994

ROLLING STOCK OF THE NARROW GAUGE

1. Four wheel railcar trailer R1 of the Estrategicos y Secundarios de Alicante at Alicante, July 1959.
(K E Hartley)

2. 'BB' 2nd class bogie coach of the FC San Feliu - Gerona at San Feliu, June 1958.
(K E Hartley)

3. Early 'Craven' 4 wheel coach and later Spanish-built 4 wheeler of the Olot - Gerona Railway at Gerona, June 1958.
(K E Hartley)

A NOTE ON THE SPANISH TEXT

From being a country where interest in railway and locomotive history was minimal, and railway publications virtually unknown, Spain has (within the last fifteen years) 'discovered' its railway heritage, and has set an example that other countries might well envy. Several magazines now flourish, and numerous books (in Spanish, Basque and Catalan languages) have been published, documenting railways on a national and local level.

Surprisingly however, apart from the translation of *'Steam on the Sierra'* published recently there has been no country-wide historical survey of the narrow gauge. On the advice of our many Spanish friends - without whose help and hospitality over the years this book would not have been as complete as it is - we have decided to include a Spanish language version of the main text, as a courtesy to those Spanish readers not fluent in English, but who wish to learn more about their rich narrow gauge heritage. The Spanish text has been prepared by Dr Mike Bent and Estela Ojeda, to whom our grateful thanks are extended.

This 'bilingual' edition is the first under the Plateway Press imprint. The increased anticipated sale has enabled additional copies of the book to be printed, so keeping the cover price down to a level no higher than would have been charged if the 'bilingual' text had not been included.

LIST OF ABBREVIATIONS/LISTA DE ABREVIATURAS

AHV	Altos Hornos de Vizcaya
ESTADO	Explotación de Ferrocarriles por el Estado
FC	Ferrocarril (Railway)
FEVE	Ferrocarriles (del Estado) de Vía Estrecha
HUNOSA	Hulleras del Norte SA
MACOSA	Material y Construcciones SA, Valencia
MAN	Maschinenfabrik Augsburg-Nürnberg AG
MTM	La Maquinista Terrestre y Maritima, Barcelona
NBL	North British Locomotive Co. Ltd.
OHW	overhead wire electric
O&K	Orenstein & Koppel
RENFE	Red Nacional de los Ferrocarriles Españoles
SACM	Société Alsacienne de Constructions Mécaniques
SECN	Sociedad Española de Construcción Naval, Bilbao
SLM	Schweizerische Locomotiv- und- Maschinenfabrik, Winterthur

PART 1
CATALUNYA TO THE SIERRA NEVADA

Crossing the frontier from France into Catalunya (Catalonia), the present day visitor will find the Catalan language widely spoken, and used for place names, company titles etc. As this book covers principally the period when regional languages were not encouraged by central government all place names, titles, etc. are in Spanish, with a few exceptions relating to present day ownership. The same comment will apply to the Valencia region, and later to the Basque area in the north.

Gerona is our first port of call on the way from Port Bou to Barcelona, as it was a town served by three narrow gauge lines, two of which linked it with the coast and one of which penetrated inland. Most of the public railways in this book will be of metre gauge but we start with the 750mm FC de San Feliu de Guixols a Gerona, 40km long. The railway opened throughout in 1892 and closed in 1969, late enough to be visited by large numbers of British enthusiasts but not quite in time to be preserved as a tourist attraction, although it remained steam operated to the end. At least most of the locomotives have survived to be 'stuffed and mounted' in the region and these were all Krauss 0-6-2Ts, six having been built between 1890 and 1905. For a while there were also two Krauss 0-8-2Ts, a six coupled diesel, and in 1964 two compound 0-6-2Ts arrived from the Onda-Castellon system. These had also been built by Krauss in 1890.

On the other side of the broad gauge RENFE tracks at Gerona was to be found the station of the metre gauge FC de Olot a Gerona. This 55km long line was built by an English company but passed into Spanish ownership in 1909. Work had started in 1895 from Amer, and Gerona was reached in 1898, but it took until 1911 to reach Olot. The first locomotives were 0-6-2Ts from Falcon of Loughborough, and these were followed by 2-6-0Ts from St. Leonard of Liège between 1910-12. By the time enthusiasts reached the line most traffic was in the hands of four 2-6-2Ts, Nos 21-24, built by MTM in 1926. The arrival of a pair of standard ESTADO Billard railcars on the scene in 1959 failed to save the line, which finally closed in 1969.

As previously stated, there was once a trio of narrow gauge lines serving Gerona but the first to be commenced was the earliest to close. The 750mm FC de Flassá a Palamós, Gerona y Bañolas ultimately linked Gerona with the coast but was built to facilitate the export of cork to France by coastal vessel. Gerona (50km) was not reached until 1921 and the Bañolas branch (14km) opened in 1928. Locomotives, the earliest of which were steam tramway types, were a varied lot, mostly 0-4-0Ts and 0-6-0Ts from various German builders. The most modern were two 0-6-0Ts from Euskalduna in 1928. The railway experimented with railcars from Krupp in 1928 but these were withdrawn the following year. In 1931 some home made ones were tried, but all had disappeared in favour of conventional steam traction by the 1950s. With steep gradients and much roadside running, the railway only lasted until 1956, and it was indeed fortunate that my first visit to Spain in 1953 enabled me to enjoy a journey over it!

Before leaving Gerona a look at services over these three lines in 1954 and ten years later may be of interest. In 1954, Olot was served by five trains a day, the journey time being just over two hours by the fastest trains (which omitted three or four halts). Mixed trains took just over 2½ hours with 16 intermediate stops. According to the timetable, only four trains returned, one less mixed than in the opposite direction, and the footnotes explained that all trains connected at Gerona with the MZA line, the publishers apparently not having bothered to alter the typesetting since formation of the RENFE in 1941! By 1965 railcars had arrived and did the journey in 90 minutes, also providing some short workings on market days. In fact the timetable had become considerably more complicated, but was probably more closely tailored to local needs. Across the broad gauge tracks the Gerona-San Feliu offered five trains daily, taking around two hours, and this situation was little changed ten years later. On the Palamós line it took 2 hours 20 minutes to cover 50km on the fastest of the two daily through trains and 50 minutes for the 16km from Gerona to Bañolas, served thrice daily.

Moving along the coast to Barcelona the city had in 1953 almost everything a transport enthusiast could desire. There were tramways and underground railways, both offering services on two gauges, three funiculars, a travelator (predating the one at Bank station in London and certainly the first one I had ever seen, although nowadays they are quite commonplace, particularly at airports). There was a cableway from the harbour to Montjuich, but this was out of use since the Civil War, although later returned to service. Unusually for Europe, there were double deck buses, trams and trolleybuses, and railways of three different gauges. By far the largest narrow gauge system in Catalonia has always been the metre gauge Compañía General de FFCC Catalanes (CGFC) which was formed by the amalgamation of a number of smaller companies and had offered since 1926 1500V dc electrified suburban services into the centre of the city, terminating beneath the Plaza de España. These only extended 11km and were worked for 30 years by four locomotives, but the main line continued on into the mountains to finally reach Guardiola, a distance of 132km. There were a number of branches, some industrial, and heavy coal traffic from the interior to Barcelona docks. A curiosity of the main line at the time of which we are writing was that as the concession for the section between Manresa and Olvan expired before the sections on either side of it this part of the railway was worked by the ESTADO organisation with locomotives lettered MO and kept at Sallent. The coaches of Barcelona-Guardiola trains worked through but changed locomotives at both Manresa and Olvan because of this. Motive power ranged from small MTM built 0-6-0Ts through Belgian built 2-6-0Ts and 2-6-2Ts (four of the latter built in 1948) to eight Garratts built by St. Leonard of Liège in the 1920s. The ESTADO section had four of the Garratts and also two 2-4-4-0Ts originally with the Swiss Rhaetian Railways, besides other types. Diesel locomotives appeared in the mid 1950s but traffic declined and the main line north of Manresa closed in 1973. The CGFC ceased to exist in 1976 when FEVE took over until in 1979 the system became part of the Ferrocarriles de la Generalitat de Catalunya (Provincial Government Railways).

In the 1960s a start was made on extending the electrification with Martorell being reached in 1968, Monistrol in 1971, and Manresa (63km) in 1984. The passenger branch from Martorell to Igualada (37km) remains diesel worked, as does the always freight only Súria line from Manresa (13km) and a new freight link to Sallent (7½km). A new link to Barcelona port has also been constructed, adding a further 12km. Salt and potash are the principal freight traffic today, handled by Alsthom BoBo diesels dating back to the late 1950s, which since 1990 have been joined by three Macosa built CoCos. Diesel and electric passenger units were modernised in the 1980s when brand new electric stock was also obtained. One of the original 1926 electric locomotives is preserved in working order, as is one of the line's many 0-6-0Ts (No 31) and 2-6-2T No 22 from the Gerona-Olot railway. These see very rare use, usually double heading, on specials, and many other steam locomotives are 'stuffed and mounted' in the area.

The CGFC connected with two other railways on the journey from Barcelona to Guardiola. One of these, the Montserrat Rack Railway, was worked by the grandly named Sociedad de FFCC de Montaña a Grandes Pendientes, a company also operating the Ribas-Núria rack line which we shall come to shortly. The Montserrat line was 8½km long, linking Monistrol (Norte) with the monastery. It was of metre gauge and opened between 1892 and 1905 with five Cail built 0-4-2Ts. Three further 0-4-2Ts were acquired in 1921/23, all SLM built. Two were new, while the third was obtained second-hand from the Gornergrat Railway in Switzerland. The railway operated at a loss from 1947 onwards and despite considering modernisation, particularly after a disastrous accident in 1953, the company decided it could no longer carry on and closed the railway in 1957. For many years afterwards the locomotives remained in their shed but fairly recently a number of them have been cosmetically restored and are preserved as 'monuments' locally. In particular, the Automobile Club of Catalonia financed restoration of a locomotive and two coaches which are displayed at Monistrol (Catalanes) station.

In 1955 I travelled to the end of the CGFC line at Guardiola and was astonished to find in the roadway outside a 600mm gauge train waiting to depart. This railway was in the timetable but I had assumed it to be a metre gauge extension of the Catalanes system. Only 12km long, it was operated by the Asland Cement Company and passengers were very much a sideline, the one coach being tacked onto the end of long and dusty cement trains. The railway was opened in 1908 by no less a person than King Alfonso XIII, but public services started in 1914 between Guardiola and Pobla de Lillet, with the 2km extension to Castellar d'en Huch opening in 1924. It was very much a roadside tramway and the motive power consisted mainly of O & K 0-4-0Ts. The railway closed in 1963 and although enthusiasts from Barcelona have hopes of reopening a section of what was the last Spanish 600mm gauge public passenger carrying railway, little progress appears to have been made to date, and the area would appear to be totally unsuitable for such a venture.

For those coming from France via the La Tour de Carol/Puigcerdà route it was possible to leave the Barcelona bound train at Ripoll and take a taxi over the mountains to Guardiola, thence reaching Barcelona over the metre gauge. Travellers over this route should first have stopped off at Ribas de Fresser to visit the metre gauge rack and adhesion line to Núria, built by the same company as the Montserrat Rack Railway but electrified from the outset in 1931 at 1500V dc. Two Montserrat steam locomotives were used during construction and today one is preserved here, although not in working order. The railway is 12½km long, ABT system, and Núria at 1965m, claims to be the highest railway station in Spain. The original four locomotives were 3-axle machines from Switzerland and the coaches were German built. Little changed until the 1980s by which time modernisation was badly needed and leisure traffic (skiing in winter and hiking in summer) had grown considerably. The Catalan Provincial Government (Generalitat) was persuaded to take a 70% interest in the Company and in 1986 the railway was integrated into the Ferrocarriles de la Generalitat de

MAP 1. EASTERN SPAIN

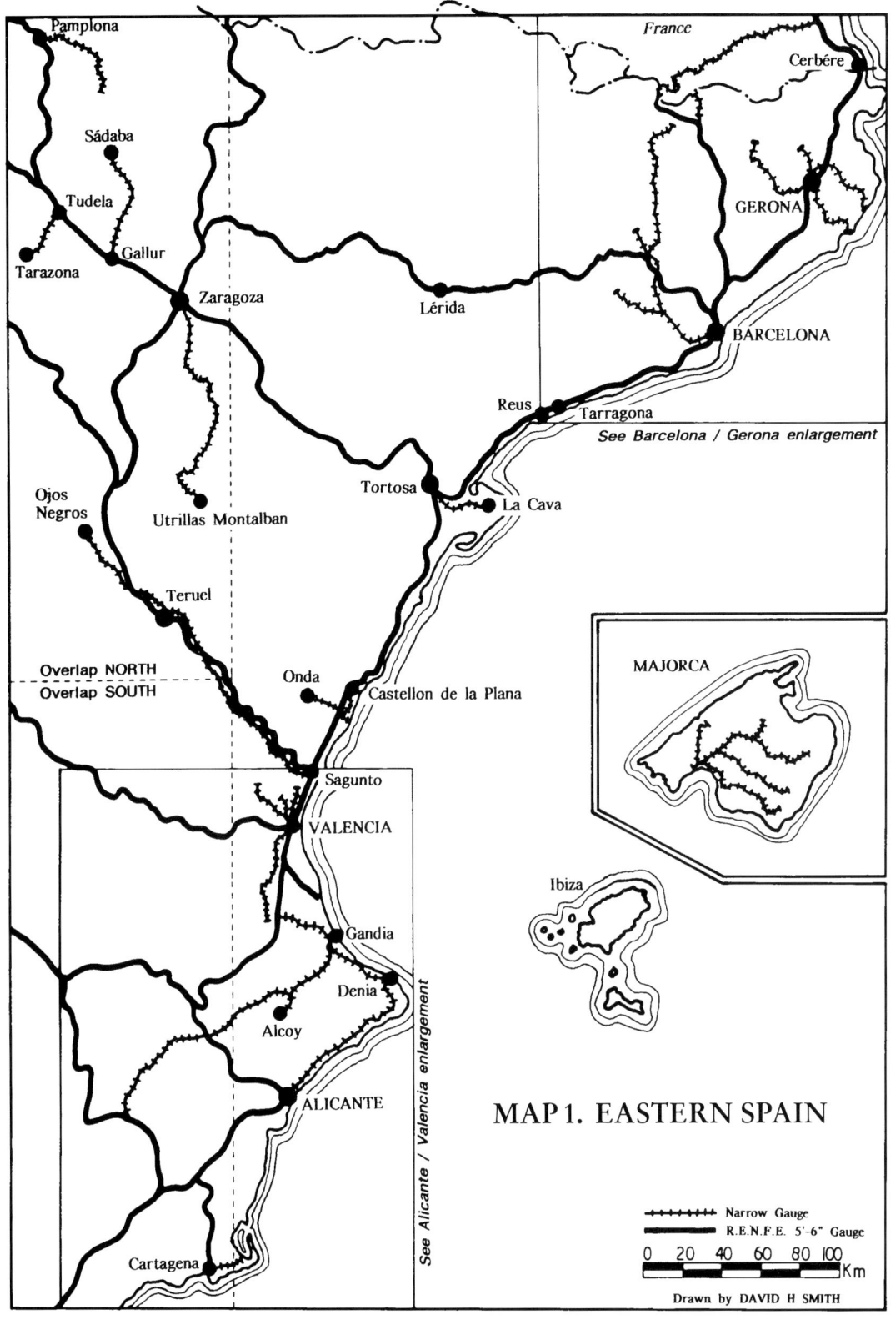

MAP 2. GERONA / BARCELONA

Drawn by DAVID H SMITH

In 1960 an overnight ferry from Barcelona would take the traveller to Palma, Mallorca. The 3ft gauge FC de Mallorca was still intact and operating by a mixture of steam locos and diesel railcars. CAF-Besain car A4 poses at Palma with the morning train to Felanitx on 10 June 1960. *(Mike Swift)*

4. San Feliu - Gerona: on 4 April 1965 No.4 pauses at Llagostera with the 1.25pm 'mixto' from San Feliu. It has travelled 19 kilometres in 55 minutes and climbed over 100 metres. The first coach is from the Onda - Castellon Railway, where it was built as a railcar trailer in 1925. The station building here still exists as a (non railway) museum. *(Author)*

5. On 25 May 1953 No.1, another Krauss 0-6-2T, is ready to leave San Feliu for Gerona. *(Author)*

6. On 25 May 1953, No.4 is to be seen outside the locomotive depot at San Feliu. *(Author)*

7. In 1953 the train on which I travelled, the 7.25am 'mixto' from Gerona, was worked by No.1, seen here heading towards the coast at Llagostera. The first coach is one of three built by Linke Hoffman in 1926, a first/second composite with (a unique feature) larger, deeper windows in the first class section. Note the 'sundries' being loaded in the van, a feature of narrow gauge travel on most lines in Spain right up to the end. *(Author)*

8. Gerona - Olot: on 3 April 1965 MTM 2-6-2T No.22 is ready to leave Amer for Olot on a passenger train. The 4-wheel coaches are still in use and in the centre of the train are a modernised pair of bogie coaches (they were built with open balconies in 1913). Happily No.22 is preserved in working order at Martorell depot of the Catalan Railways. *(Author)*

9. On the same day as the preceding photograph was taken No.23, coming from Olot, passes the depot at Amer, where 2-6-0T's 6 & 9 are dumped out of use. *(Author)*

10. I never saw the 2-6-0T's in action, but No.7 is shown here at Gerona in June 1958. *(K E Hartley)*

11. Gerona - Palamós: On 24 May 1953 the afternoon train from Palamós trundles along the street as it arrives at Gerona behind 0-6-0T No.19. *(Author)*

12. On 25 May 1953 I travelled on the afternoon train behind 0-4-0T No.12, seen here at La Bisbal.
(Author)

13. Palamós shed on 25 May 1953. In the foreground is 0-6-0T No.17 (Jung 1928), behind is No.11, the only one of a batch of O&K 0-4-0T's to have been rebuilt as an 0-4-2T, and on the right Nos.12 and 16 (O&K 0-4-0T's). No.12 is preparing to work the 2pm 'correo' to Gerona, a 50km journey which is scheduled to take 3 hours 21 minutes. *(Author)*

Catalunya. Meanwhile, much of the original passenger stock had been modernised and three new 2-car units were built in Barcelona under Swiss licence in 1986. A start was made in 1989 on modernising three of the four original locomotives, and a further 2-car set was ordered in 1992, thus ensuring adequate capacity for the future. This is now the only rack railway in Spain, and its future would appear to be secure.

Returning to Barcelona, we proceed along the coast southwards through Tarragona to Salou, now well known as a holiday resort. The FC Económico de Reus a Salou opened in 1887 with a length of only 8km. All of the steam locomotives on the line came from Falcon of Loughborough, the first three steam trams and the others 0-4-0Ts. A number of goods wagons and the first 28 four-wheel coaches were also supplied by Falcon, and were very much of the tramway style. They sufficed until 1926, when the company built itself five coaches, one of which was converted briefly in 1927 to a petrol railcar. In 1932 an 0-6-2T was obtained from the Olot-Gerona line, and this had been built at Loughborough in 1899, by which time Falcon had become Brush Engineering. Some coaches and a tram locomotive were destroyed during the Civil War and a later search for second hand passenger stock was not very successful. In the 1950s coaches on the recently closed Mollerusa-Balaguer line were inspected but not found suitable, and in the 1960s one from the Montserrat Rack line was tried but soon found to be unsuitable. Another bogie coach was then tried which had originated on the ESTADO Madrid-Almorox line in 1908 but this too was not satisfactory and was passed on to Olot-Gerona in 1964. The earlier rolling stock was forced to soldier on until two ESTADO Billard railcars arrived in 1958. A Spanish built Ferrotrade railcar was obtained in 1966 but was not a great success. Despite the two ESTADO railcars the company remained privately owned and held its own against road competition but in 1970 control was obtained by a local road transport concern who finally closed the railway in 1975. The three 0-4-0Ts are all 'plinthed' in the region.

Continuing along the coast towards Valencia, along the RENFE line over which Garratts worked passenger trains such as the Barcelona-Seville 'correo' we reach the last line to be visited in Catalonia, the metre gauge FC de Tortosa a La Cava. This 27km railway was quite a latecomer to the narrow gauge scene, being opened in 1926/7 with second-hand locomotives and stock from the SVT (Valencia) and Santander-Bilbao. All three were 4-4-0Ts built by Hunslet in 1890/91 and 1906 and they were backed up by two 4-wheel railcars of antique aspect, which had to suffice until the arrival of a standard bogie Billard in 1959. Some passenger stock dated back to 1887 and must also have been second-hand, probably from the above-mentioned sources. The operating company was Ferrocarriles Económicos SA, hence the initials FESA on the locomotives. The railway closed in 1968.

We now leave Catalonia and enter the Valencian region, where rice and oranges proliferate and many Transfesa wagons are loaded to deliver fruit all over Europe. The first narrow gauge system to be encountered was at Castellon de la Plana, where the 750mm gauge FC de Onda al Grao de Castellon which ran largely through the streets of the towns, served and endeared itself to all those who were fortunate enough to see it in action. The main line, $28^{1}/_{2}$km long, ran from Grao de Castellon (port) through the town of Castellon de la Plana to Onda, and was opened between 1888 and 1890. A branch from Villareal to Burriana, $10^{1}/_{2}$km, was added in 1907. The motive power consisted of 0-6-0Ts and 0-6-2Ts from Krauss in 1888/90, the 0-6-2Ts being 2 cylinder compounds. Much of the early rolling stock was Spanish built, 4 wheelers with end balconies. Bogie petrol railcars with trailers were tried (as on other lines) in 1927 but these were not a great success and (again as on other lines) later became coaches. The trailers survived to be passed on to the San Feliu-Gerona after closure, along with two of the compound 0-6-2Ts. A few bogie coaches came from the Gerona-Palamós line after closure and also their two Euskalduna 0-6-0Ts. The system had been operated by the ESTADO since 1931 but as road traffic increased losses mounted and projected electrification was abandoned. Unusually for such lines there were turntables at Grao and Onda, and the workshops at Grao were so well equipped that they dealt with locomotives from other ESTADO lines in the region, including those from Cartagena-Los Blancos of 1067mm gauge. Although refurbished on arrival it is not thought that the 0-6-0Ts from Gerona entered service before closure of the railway in 1963.

We now come to the first purely industrial railway to feature in this book. Between Castellon and Valencia the large steelworks of the Altos Hornos de Vizcaya company at Sagunto had an extensive metre gauge internal network making use of both steam and electric traction. The internal steam stock was extremely varied, much of it second-hand, and included two ex Alcoy-Gandía 2-6-2Ts, an ex-Vascongados 4-4-0T, an ex-Rhaetian Railways, Switzerland 2-6-2T and three locomotives from the Valencian Suburban Railways. No steam locomotives appear to have been new to Sagunto, only two had been built after the turn of the century, and the most modern had come from the AHV works in Bilbao where it had been built in 1941. Thus, apart from three Dübs 4-6-0Ts built in 1897 ex the Santander-Bilbao Railway, there were only two other 'pairs' of locomotives, the rest being 'one-offs'. Happily, visitors were welcome and given conducted tours on prior request.

If the steelworks was interesting, the method of keeping it supplied with ore was even more so. The Compañía Minera de Sierra Menera linked the mines at Ojos Negros with the works by means of a 204km long metre gauge railway which for much of the distance was in sight of the RENFE main line between Valencia and Zaragoza. Reaching a summit of over 1000m above sea level near Puerto de Escandón the railway needed large motive power and when it opened in 1907 North British provided a fleet of fourteen 480s, two further machines arriving from the same source in 1913. Also from North British between these dates came four 0-6-6-0 Mallets, and much later, in 1930, two Garratts from Euskalduna. A few 0-6-0Ts and 062Ts acted as shunters at Sagunto and at the mines, where there were also small diesel shunters. In 1964/66 five Henschel diesel hydraulics were obtained for main line work but tariff changes consequent upon the introduction of more commercial freedom of action on the RENFE resulted in a broad gauge connection being put in and the metre gauge, which must have been extremely expensive to maintain and work, finally closed in 1972, the modern diesels going to FEVE. At the beginning of the century the Central of Aragón Railway had opposed construction of the metre gauge line but when, some 70 years later, their successor at last obtained the traffic, their victory was shortlived, as recession in the steel industry and cheap imports of ore from abroad caused the rundown of the Sagunto operation and importation of ore for other northern works. The mine, although by no means worked out, was soon in difficulties, and the company went into liquidation in 1987. A trip over this railway was an experience to be savoured, Mallet and Garratt double-heading being usual over the most heavily graded section in steam days.

Back on the coast, the city of Valencia once had three separate companies operating metre gauge suburban lines. There was the line from Jesús station to Villanueva de Castellon, 52^1/$_2$km, on which the first section was opened in 1893 and Villanueva was reached in 1915. On the northern side of the city the SVT had several short routes opened between 1888 and 1893 and the Valencia a Villanueva del Grao was a 6km steam tramway until converted to electric traction in 1900. In 1911 the SVT, which had already taken over the Villanueva del Grao line, was being worked by a French company and the Compañía de Tranvías y Ferrocarriles de Valencia (CTFV) was formed in 1917.

The Villanueva de Castellon line was also taken over by the CTFV in 1946 by which time electrification of the system had started and was completed in 1955. Returning to the SVT, their system was being electrified in the 1920s, when their fleet of Hunslet 4-4-0Ts and 0-6-0Ts was disposed of, some going to the line on the other side of the city and being reunited under one ownership in 1946. The Villanueva de Castellon line had gone in for Kerr Stuart and Avonside 0-6-0Ts and also had early railbuses and steeple cab electrics for shunting. Most of the steam was scrapped in the late 1950s and the CTFV was taken over by the ESTADO organisation in 1964. Under their management the system became rather run down and in 1988 was taken over by local government, who formed the Ferrocarriles de la Generalitat Valenciana (FGV). Recently, much money has been spent on connecting the two hitherto separate systems by tunnelling and a modern suburban light rail system has been created. Unfortunately, through working between all the northern and southern suburbs of the city is still not possible as the old companies used a voltage of 600/650V dc and in the 1980s part of the system was modernised to use 1500V dc. After the opening of the cross city tunnel early in October 1988 four lines or routes were designated, line 1 trains working through from Bétera to Villanueva and line 2 trains linking Liria with Torrent. The remaining two lower voltage lines were line 3 from Puente de Madera (Pont de Fusta nowadays) to Rafelbuñol and line 4 to Grao, this latter service being extended from Puente de Madera to Ademus, reversing at the former (a terminal station) and continuing along the old surface route vacated by Bétera and Liria trains to a bay platform at Ademus. However, line 4 was closed at the end of 1990 for conversion to a 9km light rail route. It was planned that this work would be completed by the end of 1993 and for the time being it will still offer interchange at Ademus, although within two years or so a new cross city tunnel for line 3 will cause the interchange to be resited at Benimaclet. Later, a totally new line 5 is projected. The motley collection of old rolling stock (including ex Belgian Vicinal material) has now given way to modern LRVs, forty articulated sets having been built in Spain in 1986 and 1990. There are also ten Babcock & Wilcox built 3-car sets of 1981, these being standard FEVE types modernised and equipped for 1500V operation. The Rafelbuñol line uses trainsets built in 1952 but modernised in 1982 and 1989, usually worked as a power car and trailer. Finally, for the new line 4 low floor LRVs have been ordered from Siemens-Duewag and will be operated under 750V dc overhead equipment.

Leaving Valencia in the 1950s on board a 2 or 3 axle double-deck coach of the RENFE (needless to say not at all like the ones introduced for Madrid suburban services in 1990) a local train would deliver the enthusiast to Carcagente, where he could make the connection with the metre gauge Carcagente-Denia railway. As will be seen, this had physical connections enabling one to travel on the metre gauge tracks of three other companies, and at one time had almost formed part of a metre gauge link between Alicante and Valencia. The Carcagente-Denia was the first metre gauge railway in Spain, being opened in 1864 with animal traction between Carcagente and Gandía (35^1/$_2$ km in 3 hours). The extension to Denia opened in 1884, by which time the motive power had been improved, after all the length was now

14. Compañia General de los FFCC Catalanes: in 1953 electric traction only extended from the underground terminus beneath the Plaza de España, Barcelona to San Baudillo, where 2-6-2T No.202 has just taken over the train. *(Author)*

15. On 13 October 1957 2-6-0T No.16 arrives at Martorell Empalme with an Igualada to Barcelona train. *(L G Marshall)*

16. A freight working hauled by Garratt No.104 pauses at Martorell Empalme on 14 May 1958.
(D W Winkworth)

17. Garratt No.103, showing the cylindrical tank at the front end. Seen at Manresa on 1 April 1961.
(Author)

18. One of the original four electric locomotives is seen in action in March 1965 at San Baudillo.
(J Wiseman)

19. The CGFC passed to FEVE in 1976 but its salvation came with transfer to the Ferrocarils de la Generalitat de Catalunya (FGC) in 1979. Catalan station names are now in evidence, Empalme has now become Enllaç. In December 1991 one of the MAN built diesel cars of 1966, which were rebuilt from 1986 onwards, is working the Igualada service. Alongside is one of the three new diesel locomotives for freight traffic, built in 1990 by Macosa. *(Author)*

MAP 3. SOUTHERN SPAIN

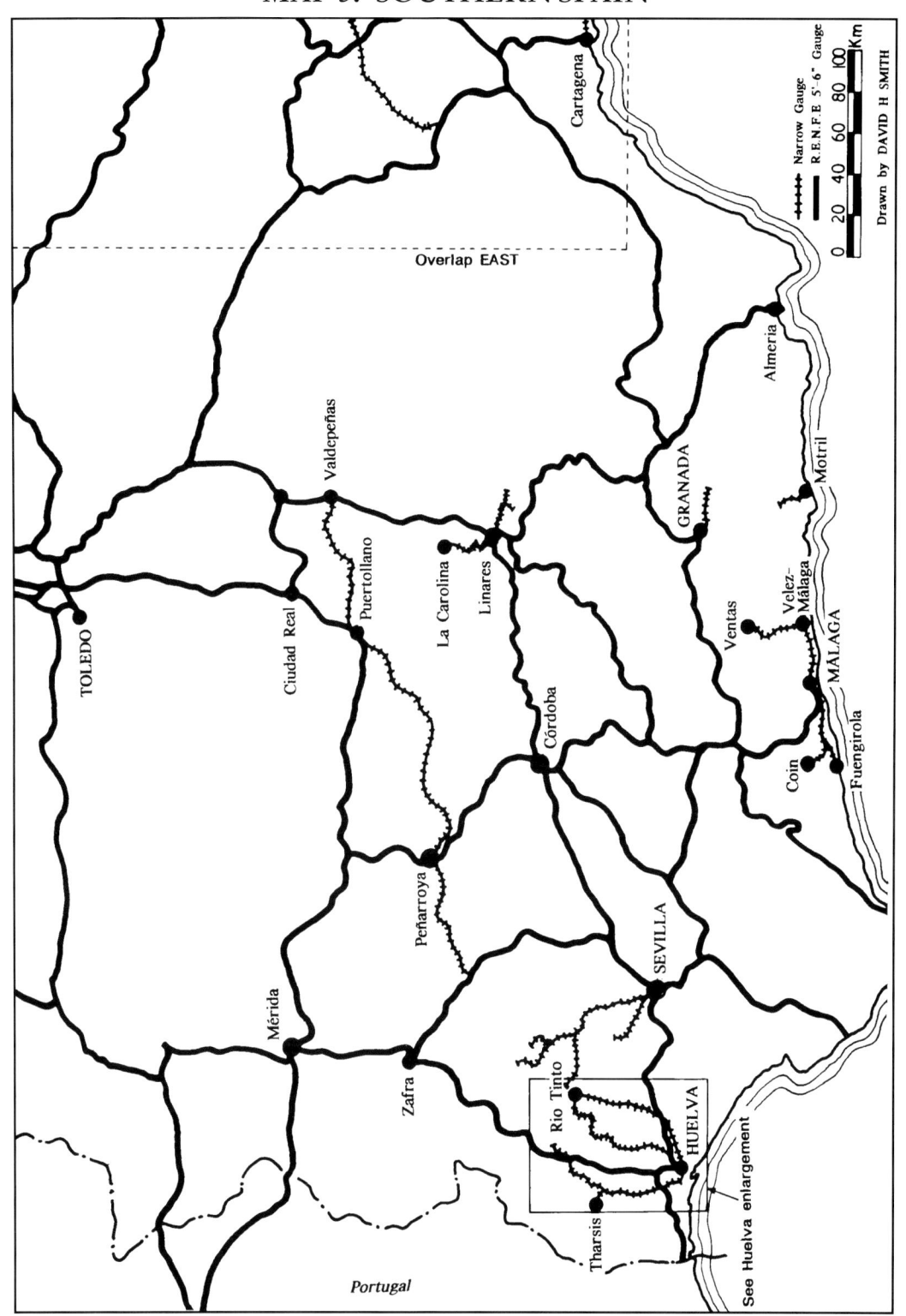

MAP 4. ALICANTE / VALENCIA

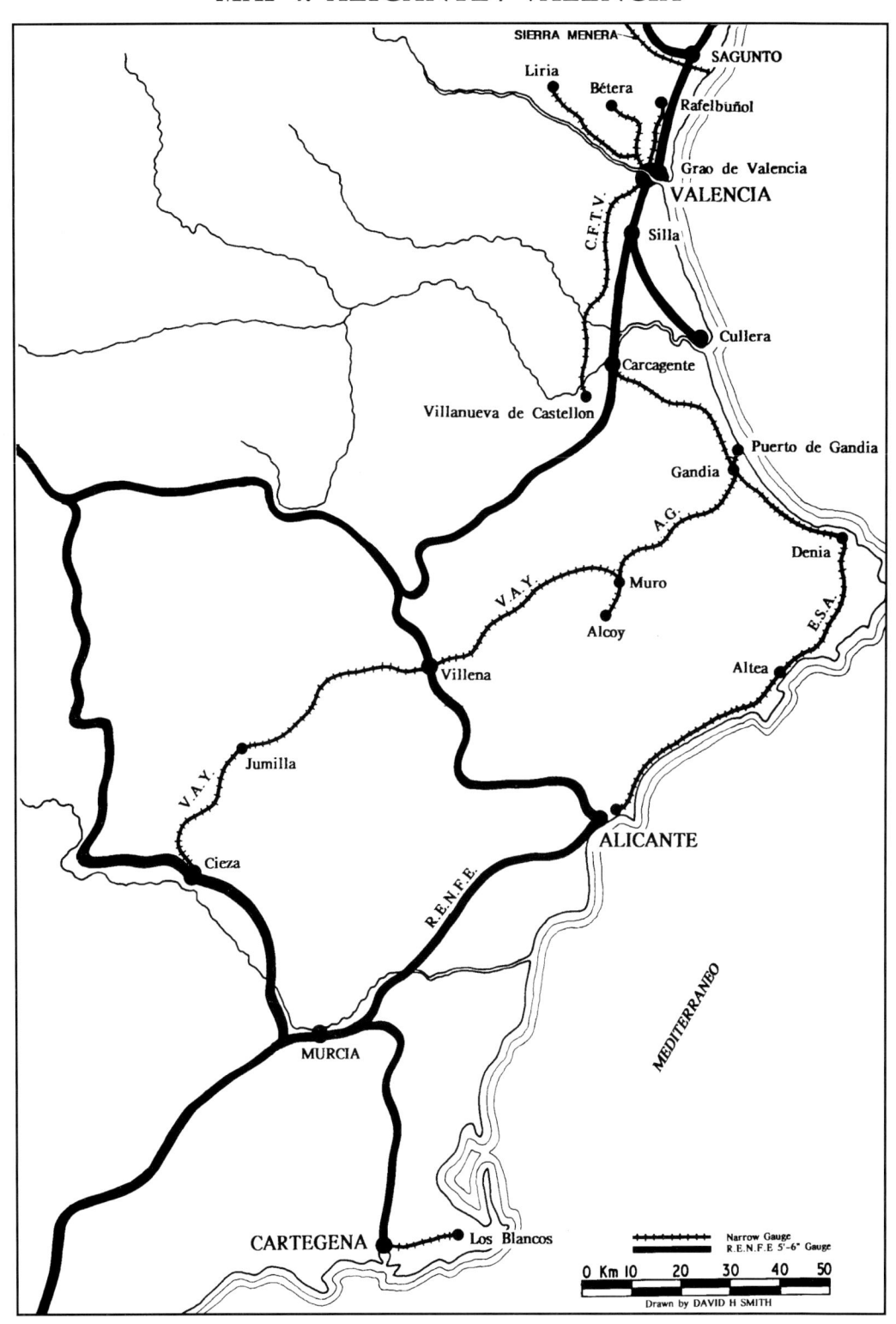

65½km! It is claimed that 2 axle double deck coaches were used in the early days, and lasted into the 20th century! It was formerly owned by the Norte and its predecessor, the Almansa-Valencia-Tarragona Railway, but passed to the ESTADO in 1942. Black Hawthorn 4-4-0Ts were the first locomotives, followed by Belgian 0-6-0Ts and a couple of oddments from the nearby Silla-Cullera line when this was broad-gauged in 1935. Two early double ended railcars added to the delights of travel over this route until superseded by standard ESTADO bogie cars in 1958. Diesel locomotives also made their appearance about this time and in 1959 a through service was introduced to Alicante, over the tracks of the Alicante-Denia Railway, by then also part of the ESTADO organisation. This journey of 160km took 3 hours 40 minutes. Despite these improvements, Carcagente to Gandía was closed in 1969, and in 1972 an extension of the RENFE Cullera branch reached Gandía. Instead of the through narrow gauge link between Alicante and Valencia once envisaged by this route, the broad gauge had triumphed over at least a section of it! The narrow gauge was left with a 124km line between Gandía and Alicante, via Denia, and offered quite a frequent service along the developing Costa Blanca. Nonetheless, the Gandía-Denia section closed in 1974.

The Compañía de los FFCC Estratégicos y Secundarios de Alicante (ESA) built the Alicante-Denia Railway (93½km) which opened in 1914/15. Its entire steam stock consisted of 2-6-0Ts, all built in 1913 by Hanomag and MTM. Railcars first arrived in 1949/50, home made by the railway with matching trailers, and these were followed by standard ESTADO Billard cars in 1958. As previously mentioned, under ESTADO control services were developed through to Carcagente, later cut back to Denia. Happily, Alicante-Denia (94km) still flourishes, and since 1988 has been operated by FGV, who run the Valencia system. There are frequent railcar services, particularly between Alicante and Benidorm, and the locomotive hauled 'Limón Expres' is operated from Benidorm for tourists, some of the open balcony passenger stock having come from Manresa-Olvan, and some from the Carcagente-Denia, rebuilt in 1987. Motive power is diesel, the railway having in stock in 1992 two diesel-electric BoBos built by Babcock & Wilcox under Alsthom licence in 1959 and two Batignolles/Besain diesel-hydraulic 0-6-0s of about the same vintage. One of the latter is depicted on a commercial postcard of the 'Limón Expres' but, sadly, steam power does not seem to have been considered for this service. The railcars are eight two-car (92 seat) MAN built sets dating from 1967, but rebuilt in 1984.

Retracing our steps to Gandía, the Carcagente-Denia connected there with the FC de Alcoy al Puerto de Gandía, an English company which built the 53km long line in 1893 and managed all its life with eight Beyer Peacock 2-6-2Ts of 1890/91, two of which went to Sagunto steelworks in 1947. There was a Manning Wardle 0-6-0T, probably used on construction work as it was built in 1890, but this went to the next railway to be described, the VAY, in 1920. At Gandía the tracks of the two metre gauge lines crossed on the level and separate stations were maintained although there was physical connection. The Alcoy-Gandía closed in 1969, still using the original locomotives and coaches built in previous century. It had been worked by the ESTADO since 1963 but had escaped modernisation, resources having been concentrated on the more viable coastal line. One of the locomotives, No 7, is preserved as a monument outside the fine new RENFE station at Gandía.

On arrival at Alcoy it was possible to take a railcar over the long (102km) FFCC Económicos de Villena a Alcoy y Yecla (VAY). The tracks of this railway joined those of the Alcoy-Gandía at Muro, but trains always worked to and from Alcoy over the AG tracks, a distance of some 10km. The VAY was opened between 1884 and 1909 and also worked the FC de Jumilla a Cieza (32km) opened in 1921. The locomotive stock consisted mainly of German built 0-6-0Ts, although there were two Couillets, all built in 1883. When the Jumilla-Cieza opened two Vulcan (USA) 2-6-2Ts arrived, plus the previously mentioned Manning Wardle from the Alcoy-Gandía. The first railcars arrived in 1929 and handled most of the passenger traffic in later days, often hauling ancient silver painted 4 wheel coaches. The ESTADO took over operation in 1965 and the railway closed in 1969, a bad year for the four systems which together covered 348km serving the provinces of Valencia, Murcia, and Alicante. It was in fact a bad year for ESTADO controlled lines in general, the investment in railcars and diesel locomotives in 1958/59 had not arrested decline in all cases, and a more ruthless course was now being taken.

And now for a change of gauge! The FC de Cartagena a La Unión y Los Blancos was of 1067mm (3ft 6in) gauge and was originally a British company, the Cartagena and Herrerías Steam Tramways Co. Ltd. The first section opened in 1874, and Los Blancos was reached in 1897, the final section having been built by a Belgian company. Financial troubles came early with a slump in local mining activities and the line has been worked by the ESTADO since 1931. In its heyday the railway had a large stock of locomotives, including Hunslet and Manning Wardle 0-4-0STs and 0-6-0STs, and 0-6-0Ts. There were also six wheel vertical boiler Sentinels, which were derelict but still in existence in the 1960s. A diesel hydraulic and two standard railcars arrived in 1960 but in 1972/73 the line was regauged to metre, and reopened to a new terminal at Los Nietos (19km) in 1976, the El Estrecho-Los Blancos section being abandoned. Today this is a railcar worked passenger line.

20. Manresa - Olván: on 1 April 1961 a visit to the ESTADO depot at Sallent produced the sight of most of the steam fleet inactive, including the Garratts, the remaining ex Swiss 2-4-4-0T and some of the 0-6-0T's. An Alsthom diesel-electric of 1967 was working the passenger service. Illustrated is the ex-Rhaetian Railways Mallet (SLM 1902). *(Author)*

21. One of the Trubia built 2-8-2T's of 1935 allocated to the railway. Ten of these were built for El Ferrol-Gijon, a railway which was not completed until 1972, by which time steam traction was obsolete. *(Author)*

It is a long but very scenic journey to the next point of narrow gauge interest, which is the city of Málaga. The Compañía de los FFCC Suburbanos de Málaga (FSM) operated metre gauge lines extending both eastwards and westwards from the city, in one direction serving Vélez-Málaga (36km) reached in 1908. Until the late 1950s this line continued on into the mountains over a rack section to reach Ventas de Zafarraya (68km) in 1922. In the opposite direction the line to Coín (40km) was completed in 1913. Before 1934 the Málaga-Fuengirola service (30km) had been operated by the FSM but was then taken over by the ESTADO organisation, whose trains had to run over 8km of FSM tracks to reach the city. FSM motive power consisted mostly of 1906 built Tubize 0-6-0Ts, the rack locomotives being supplied by SLM in 1920/24. When the ESTADO took over the Fuengirola line they imported three Falcon 0-6-0Ts of 1887/88 from the recently electrified Vasco-Navarro railway, and three Couillet 0-6-0Ts of 1886 when the TudelaTarazona was broad-gauged in 1952. Railcars arrived on the ESTADO section during their modernisation plan of 1958/59 and as the line served the rapidly expanding 'costa', including Torremolinos, it was regauged between 1971 and 1975 and is still in service as part of the RENFE, with electric multiple units offering a frequent service. Although the FSM has gone, ironically the one section of the Málaga metre gauge which it had lost to the ESTADO, presumably because it was not viable in 1934, has survived the rest of the system!

And so to Seville, where on the outskirts of the city two metre gauge mining railways came down from the interior to reach wharves on the River Guadalquivir. The longest of these served the Minas de Cala (97km) plus branches, one of which reached almost to the Río Tinto. The railway was virtually moribund by the 1950s, although prior to 1938 it had operated a passenger service. The depot was at San Juan de Aznalfarache, on the river, and reached in those days by electric tramcar from Seville. The depot of the other line was at Camas, also reached by tramway and at a point where the two railways crossed each other. The FC Aznalcóllar al Guadalquivir had some 48km of track but by the 1950s only the section between Camas and the river, dual gauge with metre gauge locomotives sometimes hauling broad gauge wagons, was in regular use. To the Minas de Cala Borsig supplied 0-4-0Ts and 0-6-4Ts but as traffic declined some were sold to other railways. On the Aznalcóllar line 0-6-2Ts from Jung and Krauss formed the motive power and on both companies all locomotives bore names.

We now head towards the Portuguese frontier and en route to Huelva is the small station of La Palma del Condado, from whence a short 600mm gauge line ran for only ten years (1921-31) to Bollullos del Condado. This was a passenger line rather than a mining one, and it is mentioned because the motive power consisted of two Hunslet 4-6-0T's, ALMONTE and BOLLULLOS, built in 1918 for the War Department. There was also a 40HP Motor Rail Simplex. The line effectively closed (service suspended due to 'lack of servicable motive power') on 8 November 1931. It still had a table number allocated in the 1954 'Guía' with the comment *no presta servicio de viajeros* (no passenger service).

A little further along the main line to Huelva the narrow gauge tracks of the Río Tinto line appear at Las Mallas and continue to Huelva. This is probably the best known of the Spanish industrial railways and the 83km long main line was opened in 1875. More locomotives were delivered to Río Tinto than to any other narrow gauge railway in Spain and apart from early Baldwin tank engines scrapped in the 1930s, all reflected the British origin of the company. There was a vast stock of 0-6-0Ts, a very jolly little Hawthorn Leslie 0-4-0 Crane Tank, two Garratts and of course the 1953 built 2-6-0s which did most of the main line work in latter days. If this interesting line is not more fully dealt with here it is because the full history was set out in the Plateway Press book devoted to the railway published in 1991.

Before Huelva is the small town of San Juan del Puerto, from whence a railway of 1067mm gauge extended inland to Valverde, Buitrón and Zalamea. The railway has a long history, dating back to 1868, passenger services having been inaugurated a few years later in 1874. In the early days it was British owned by the United Alkali Co. later to become part of ICI. The passenger service ceased in 1934 and as the mines became worked out the railway declined until in 1942 the ESTADO took over. Passenger services were later reintroduced, and in 1954 the timetable showed three daily trains between San Juan and Buitrón (36km), and one daily mixed train between Valverde and Zalamea (21km). At Zalamea Río Tinto passenger trains carried on to Nerva over their tracks, which were of course the same gauge. By 1965 railcars had arrived and worked between San Juan and Zalamea, but by 1968 the railway had closed. The British built steam locomotives, all named, were Kitson 0-6-0Ts and 4-6-0Ts, with a pair of Andrew Barclay 4-6-0Ts as well. The most modern dated from 1908!

We now come to a railway which, after Río Tinto, was probably the best known of the mining lines in this area, the Tharsis Railway. The Tharsis Copper and Sulphur Company had its concession granted in 1866 and its port is at Puntal de la Cruz on the river Odiel, hard by the town of Huelva, a town well known to railway enthusiasts if not to tourists although we all should know that Columbus sailed from nearby Palos in 1492 to discover America. Although long before railways, the mineral wealth of the sierras inland from Huelva had already been exploited for more than 1000 years by then. Reverting to the railway, the gauge is unusually 1219mm, more easily recognisable as 4ft, the same

22. Montserrat Rack Railway: on 27 May 1953 No.2 is ready to leave Monistrol Norte for the ascent to the Monastery. In this year I was one of the 152,739 passengers carried but 1947 had been the record year with over 273,000 travellers. *(Author)*

23. A commercial postcard showing a train en route. The railway achieved worldwide fame when one of its crossing keepers trained his dog 'Bobi' to pose, in 'uniform', in a begging position alongside a dummy signal lever. *(Author's collection)*

24. A general view of the terminus at Montserrat, an undated photo but clearly taken on a busy day. At least four trains are present, with locomotives from Cail and SLM visible. *(Author's collection)*

MAP 5. HUELVA

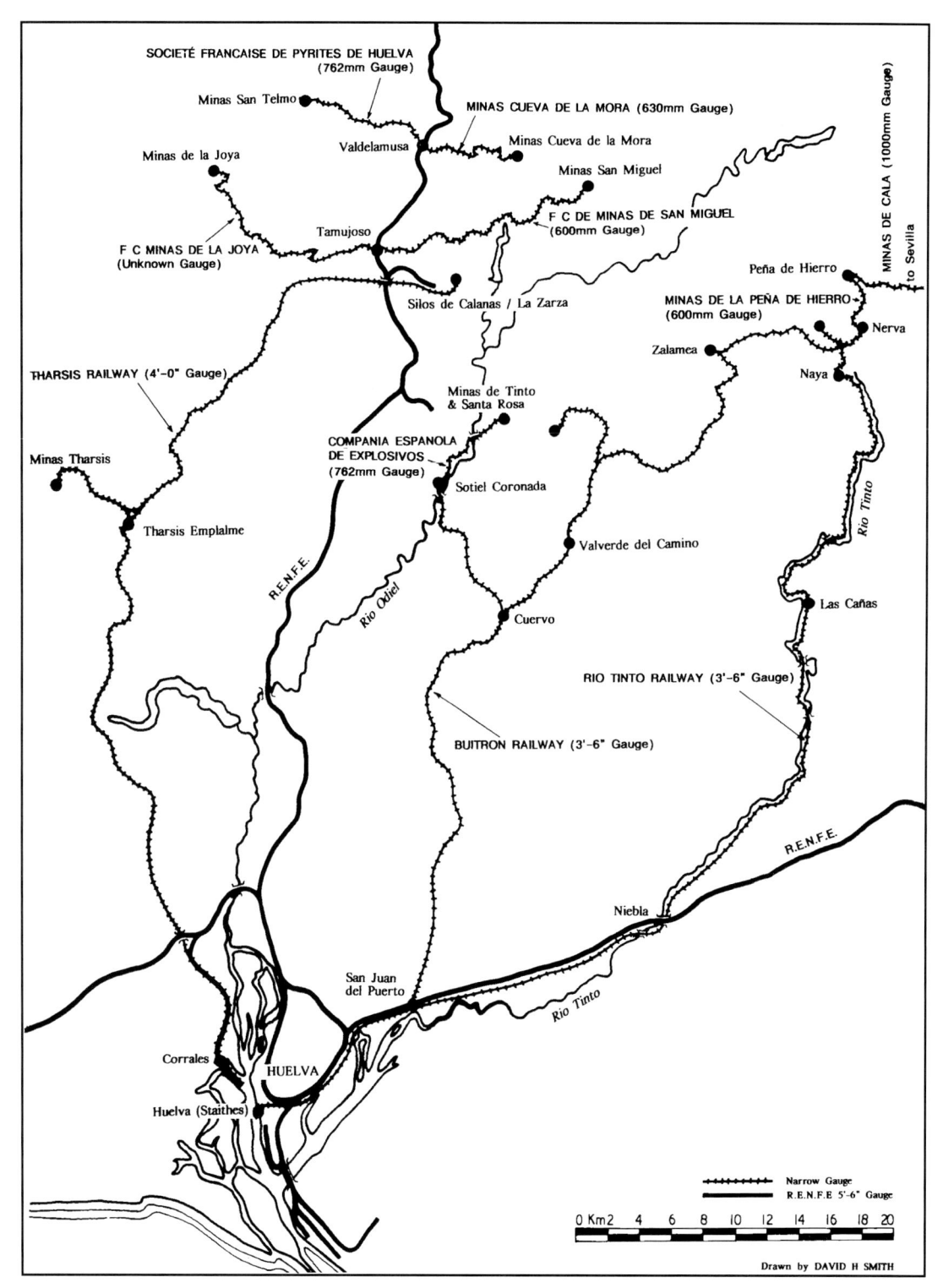

as the Glasgow underground where the company had its head office, a connection which seems tenuous at best! The main line from Tharsis to Puntal was only 46km long with a public passenger service, one train in each direction, on Mondays only! To serve the mining area which extended beyond Tharsis a standardised and relatively modern fleet was maintained, consisting of Hohenzollern built 2-8-0Ts (1923/29), North British 2-8-0Ts (1930) and 080Ts (1930/35). All were named and small diesels were also used at the mines. The early locomotives were Dübs 0-4-0Ts and 0-6-0Ts, of which No 1 ODIEL of 1867 survived. The railway remained in use in 1994 with diesel traction, including French built BoBos of 1966 vintage.

Having now followed the coastline of Spain from the French frontier to the most southerly point of the Portuguese one, we will take a brief glance inland at the mining area behind Huelva, where several 762mm gauge mining railways were to be found. The Compañía Española de Explosivos at Sotiel Coronado had ceased rail operation by the early 1960s, with only a derelict Barclay 0-4-0T remaining to be photographed. It had at one time been a British company, but the title Société Française des Pyrites de Huelva at Valdelamusa leaves no doubt as to the origin of the next line to be mentioned. By the 1960s diesels had virtually taken over from steam here and the old French and German built 0-4-0Ts and 0-6-0Ts were out of use. The railway served mines at San Telmo from whence the mineral was brought to Valdelamusa RENFE for transhipment to Huelva. On the other side of the RENFE tracks existed a short British owned line of 10km and 630mm gauge, serving mines at Cueva de la Mora. Records exist of 0-4-0T ROSALIA built by Kerr Stuart in 1902, but all trace of the railway had gone by 1964. Another 'feeder' to the broad gauge Zafra-Huelva line was the FC de Minas de San Miguel, 18km long, of 600mm gauge and with, among others, two Kerr Stuart 0-6-0Ts built in the same year as ROSALIA above. Yet another line some 14½km long connected the broad gauge here but I have no record of the gauge or stock of the FC de la Mina de la Joya.

Reverting to the 762mm gauge we will take a look at the FC del Guadiana which served the Minas de Herrerías and, unlike the others mentioned, was completely isolated from other lines of any gauge. It existed to bring ore from the mines to the Guadiana river (approx. 20km), which forms the frontier between Spain and Portugal. Three St. Leonard built 0-6-0Ts were supplied in the 1920s and formed the final steam stock, earlier locomotives having come from Black Hawthorn (0-4-0ST) and John Fowler (3 x 0-6-0STs). By the 1960s diesels had virtually taken over from steam and two Ruhrtaler ones were passed on to the San Telmo line when the railway closed in 1966. Puerto de la Laja, where the ore was discharged, was only a few kilometers from Pomerao, on the Portuguese bank of the river, where an industrial line, again completely isolated from any other railway, linked the mines with the river. This was of 1067mm gauge, about 16km long and had started out with animal traction. Because of its British associations and interesting locomotive stock, it is included as a 'guest railway' in this book. The first locomotives built in 1864 were 0-4-0WTs from Hawthorns of Leith. Other locomotives came from well known British builders such as Hunslet, Kerr Stuart, Kitson, Manning Wardle, the only eight-coupled example being a Beyer Peacock of 1898 obtained from the Río Tinto in 1926. The most modern were three Peckett 0-4-0Ts of 1952 and the railway claimed to have built an 0-4-0ST MOSQUITO at their São Domingo works in 1922. The railway closed about the same time as the one on the opposite bank of the river, which was becoming unnavigable for the ore carrying vessels.

Before leaving this interesting mining region brief mention can be made of the Minas de la Peña de Hierro, back up in the mountains near the town of Nerva, and close to the Río Tinto mines. This mine had a 600mm railway using Borsig 0-4-0Ts built in the early 1900s but its mineral was carried over Río Tinto metals to Huelva. Following a dispute over tariffs the Peña Copper Mines Ltd agreed with the Minas de Cala company to extend their branch from Minas Castillo de las Guardas to La Peña (21km), thus enabling them to use a metre gauge outlet to the Guadalquivir river near Seville. As this concession was granted for a public railway passenger services were worked and in 1921 two trains a day linked San Juan de Aznalfarache (near Seville) with Peña de Hierro, a distance of 92km. Only 11km were lacking to connect this railway to the Río Tinto and/or San Juan del Puerto lines, but of course they were of differing gauges! However, a traveller from Seville to Huelva could have made the journey by narrow gauge in a day .... a very long day with this 11km or so gap in the middle, it is true, and railway enthusiasts being thin on the ground in those days, I doubt if it was ever done. I am also unaware of how long this passenger service lasted but the Minas de la Peña owned metre gauge locomotives including a pair of Krauss built 2-8-0Ts of 1912, which later, rebuilt to 2-8-2Ts, became La Robla Railway No 120 and Santander-Bilbao Railway No 61.

It is possible that other mining railways existed, perhaps briefly, in this area, but we must now move on and having in the preceding paragraph led the reader back towards Seville the next step is to travel northwards from there towards Zafra, along which broad gauge route we could in the past have detrained at Fuente del Arco, from whence it was possible to travel 218km over the metre gauge to Puertollano, via Peñarroya. The FC Puertollano-Peñarroya (PP) had a good stock of mainly French motive power, Fives-Lille 0-6-0Ts and 0-8-0Ts built between 1894 and 1907, 2-6-0Ts from SACM in 1914, two La Meuse 2-8-0Ts and three ex-Tunisian 2-10-0s, the last named obtained in 1953 and French built in 1927. The only German was a Henschel 0-6-6-0T and almost all locomotives bore names. At Peñarroya the ENCAR coal mines had a broad gauge system (which operated passenger services) connecting with the RENFE but there was also a lead smelter with two metre gauge 0-6-0Ts. This was connected to the PP, and was owned by the mining company which had built the railway.

Back on the PP, the section from Conquista to Puertollano (50km) had been electrified at 3000V dc in 1927 due to the fierce gradients and French electric locomotives were used here until the system closed in 1970, by which time it was being operated by ESTADO/FEVE who had earlier provided the usual railcars for passenger traffic. At Puertollano was the headquarters of the company which had built the PP. The Sociedad Minera y Metalúrgica de Peñarroya (SMMP) had been formed as a French company (hence the origin of the locomotives) in 1881. They used broad gauge locomotives (again mostly French and Belgian 0-6-0Ts and 0-10-0Ts) for their coal mining operations there but had one metre gauge locomotive which had originally been in PP stock. There was also a 640mm gauge system at Mina Andrubal, with Couillet 0-6-0Ts, all part of the same organisation.

As can be imagined, this area was far from being attractive, except to railway enthusiasts, but from Puertollano a 750mm gauge line continued on across central southern Spain to Valdepeñas (on the main line from Madrid to Córdoba and Seville). The Valdepeñas-Puertollano railway was one of the most delightful in Spain. Leaving the industrial/mining area it took one on into pleasant countryside, terminating in a wine growing/agricultural district far removed from the polluted area through which one had passed. Here, at least in latter days, passengers seemed to be more important than freight, and the locomotive stock, all named, was divided into three types. There were three 0-6-0s (which had originally been built as tank engines) from Couillet in 1891/94, and two 0-4-2s from Jung in 1903, plus another 0-6-0 built by O&K in 1903. The length of the railway was 76km and in its latter days it was operated by the ESTADO, closing in 1963.

Turning southwards from Valdepeñas towards Córdoba the metre gauge Linares-La Carolina railway was another early casualty which had seen better days before the 1960s. In 1954 two trains a day were advertised, they were 'mercancías' taking two hours to cover the 39km no doubt with many delays for shunting en route. Passenger traffic faded away and the railway which had been built principally to serve lead mines, closed in 1961. Motive power consisted of four St Leonard built 0-8-0Ts of 1908.

Linares also had an interurban electric light railway system, opened in 1907 and known as the FC Eléctrico de la Loma. Metre gauge, 600V dc, the line linked Baeza-Empalme (on the main Madrid-Granada railway which avoided Linares) with Ubeda (23km) and Baeza Ciudad, the latter by means of a short 5km branch from La Yedra. The Linares town tramways had opened local routes in 1902 and in 1914 opened a link to Baeza Empalme (6½km) at the same time making a physical connection with the steam line at San Roque. Thereafter, the combined electric system was operated as one and was taken over by the ESTADO in 1936. This basically roadside tramway carried on until by the early 1950s it was in a decrepit state and, surprisingly, replacement was proposed by means of a 1500V dc light railway on a private right of way. Work began in 1953 and continued sporadically until the early 1960s, some sections of track being brought into use, many earthworks and a fine new station at Ubeda (minus track) having been completed by 1962. New trainsets were also delivered but not used as of course the old 600V cars were still trundling along. By about 1964 work had stopped, never to resume, and the whole system closed in 1966.

During my visit to this line, an incident was encountered which, although already recounted in the *Modern Tramway* in 1964, bears repetition and the description of which is repeated verbatim from that article by kind permission of the editor.

"We followed the road from Linares to Baeza-Empalme and Tres Olivas without seeing a single car in action, and after taking up a strategic position outside La Yedra an obliging goatherd deployed his flock across the tracks just as a tram was due. Unfortunately it never came, and we rounded a bend on our way to La Yedra to come upon a truly amazing sight. There was the tram, with one of its two trailers well and truly off the track, and around it milled at least a hundred Civil Guards, evidently the cause of hopelessly overloading the ancient vehicles; the trams had, contrary to Spanish Law, gone on strike in protest! Continuing on to Ubeda, we found the town full of disconsolate Guards who were supposed to be on the next tram-train to the RENFE station. Darkness was falling when we returned to Baeza-Empalme. The small village around the RENFE station had suddenly doubled in population with the belated arrival of two tram-trainloads of Civil Guards. The bars were doing a roaring trade, and some of the Guards had even muscled in on the locals' game of dominoes. One presumes that the train on which they were supposed to depart had long since gone, its reserved coaches empty.

The unfortunate draft of newly passed out trainees from Ubeda barracks were compelled to fight their way on to the already fully-loaded night express to Madrid, and one could well imagine that their immaculate appearance would be somewhat less elegant the following morning. However, it is just as well that they were not on the way to quell some insurrection, or the history of Spain might have been changed overnight by the Ubeda tram."

Another tramway which passed into the hands of the ESTADO before closure was the Granada-Sierra Nevada line of 750mm gauge. It was opened from Granada to Maitena in 1925, and was taken over by the ESTADO after it had closed in 1931. It was extended to San Juan (1160m) (21km) in the 1950s and further extensions were planned, along with ski centre developments, but despite this closure occurred in 1974.

Granada also had a metre gauge city tramway system, one long interurban line of which extended to Dúrcal (30km), from whence a long industrial cableway had continued to the coast at Motril. Here, far from any other railway system, was a metre gauge line to Puerto de Calahonda (13km), which also linked Motril town and port. At one time there may have been a passenger service here but when the area was visited in 1962 all that was found were three derelict locomotives, which appeared to have belonged to the Puerto de Motril and which may or may not have been associated with the above railway. They were an O&K 0-4-0T, an O&K 0-6-0T and a Couillet 0-4-0T of 1883.

○ ○ ○ ○ ○ ○ ○ ○ ○

Thus ends part one of this survey of the Spanish narrow gauge. **Part Two** Castile to the Biscay Coast will commence in the centre of the country, at Madrid, cover lines to the north and then follow the long metre gauge line for the length of the northern coastline to end up with what was the last significant bastion of steam traction in Spain, the Ponferrada-Villablino line.

After closure the locomotives remained in the derelict depot at Monistrol for many years, while the tracks became overgrown and the stations deteriorated. This was the scene in April 1965 before four of the locomotives were rescued. One is on display, with some carriages, at Gualba de Dalt. One is at Ribas and is illustrated on page 35.
(Author)

25. Guardiola - Castellar d'en Huch: the charm of the 600mm gauge railway is perfectly captured in this commercial postcard, showing a train passing the church at Guardiola with the terminus, situated in the road above the metre gauge CGFC station, in the background. The goods interchange is on the other side of the metre gauge and reached from the other side of the church. *(Author's collection)*

26. On 1 April 1961 0-4-0WT No.14 pauses at Pobla de Lillet, 'apartador,' where the cableway connection to the coal mines at Catllaras discharges into the wagons. *(Author)*

27. On 1 April 1961 No.14 works the train seen in the preceding photograph back towards Guardiola, and is seen leaving Pobla de Lillet. The 'roadside' character of the line is readily apparent from this view.
(Author)

28. Two months later, on 12 June 1961, No.16, the one modern locomotive on the line (Jung 1954), approaches Pobla de Lillet station en route to Castellar d'en Huch. *(D W Winkworth)*

29. Ribas de Fresser - Nuria: E4 descending from Nuria on 31 January 1982. *(J Wiseman)*

30. More snow is in evidence on 6 December 1991 at the upper terminus of Nuria. *(Author)*

31. Ex Montserrat rack railway locomotive and coach, normally kept in a locked shed at Ribas, have been brought out for the photographer. *(P Baliarda)*

32. Reus-Salou: on 12 October 1957 Falcon 0-4-0T No.5 is in action at Salou. Note the casually loaded wagon! *(L G Marshall)*

33. By 2 April 1961 all three steam locomotives are out of use at Reus and passenger workings are in the hands of a Billard railcar which had been delivered in 1958. It is seen here at Salou with three old four-wheel coaches. The expected matching trailers for the railcars never arrived, and some coaches were painted in the two-tone green livery of the Billards. *(Author)*

34. A rare gathering of Loughborough-built steam locomotives, Nos.5, 6 and 4, stand out of use at Reus on 2 April 1961. *(Author)*

35. Tortosa - La Cava: in April 1961 Hunslet 4-4-0T No.1 poses for the photographer at Tortosa, but the service is being worked by railcars. *(Author)*

36. On 13 June 1961 a later visitor is fortunate to find steam back in action. No.1 is seen at Amposta, en route from La Cava to Tortosa. The loco is now preserved in a park at Tortosa.   *(D W Winkworth)*

37. On the same date another 4-4-0T, No.3, arrives at Tortosa with a train from La Cava.
(D W Winkworth)

38. Castellon de la Plana - Onda: street running was the norm on this 750mm gauge line, which I visited on 4 and 5 April 1961. No.9, an 0-6-0WT from Hohenzollern in 1905, was the only one of its type on the line and is here seen approaching the central square of Castellon, assisted by the local traffic police.
(Author)

39. At Grao, No.9 takes a rest, and No.8 is seen arriving on a one coach 'shuttle' from Castellon.
(Author)

40. Heading back from Grao to Castellon are Nos 3 and 9. The large bogie coaches were built as early railcar trailers and some of them subsequently saw service on the San Feliu - Gerona line. *(Author)*

41. No.1 poses with the stationmaster and train crew at Burriana. *(Author)*

42/43. Finally, two commercial postcards of this most attractive system. The Plaza de la Paz, the main square of Castellon, seen with a train travelling away from Grao, and a passenger train leaving the port (Grao). Normally services terminated at Grao station, but on Sundays and holidays were sometimes extended through the port area to the beach. The port is principally served by broad gauge RENFE tracks, the narrow gauge being, at least in its latter days, mainly a passenger operation.

(Both, Author's collection)

44. AHV Steelworks, Sagunto: No.110 CASTELLON, exhibiting the classic clean lines of a Hunslet design, is seen in action against a semi-rural backdrop on 21 March 1961. No.110 came here from the Valencian Suburban Railways around 1929. *(L G Marshall)*

45. One of the traditions inherited by Spain from British practice was the naming of locomotives, and all engines on this system were named. No.212 ALCOY was built by Beyer Peacock in 1891 and was one of a pair obtained from the Alcoy - Gandia Railway about 1947. *(Author)*

46. No.208 ZUMAYA was a 4-4-0T built by Nasmyth Wilson in 1900 and second-hand from the Vascongados Railway in Northern Spain. Note the shutter on the cab window, designed to protect the crew when working in exposed positions in the foundry. *(Author)*

47. Beyer Peacock No.212, already described, is a classic 'passenger' type, and looks slightly out of place in an industrial setting. Neverthless like all locomotives on this system she is well kept, in this view taken on 21 March 1961. *(L G Marshall)*

48. No.209 VIZCAYA, an 0-4-0WT built by AHV Bilbao in 1941, is a true steelworks design - note the huge 'dumb' bufferbeam. An electric locomotive can be glimped in the background. *(Author)*

49. The electric locomotives were of considerable interest. Pictured on 21 March 1961 are 1501, built by Siemens in 1889 and therefore older than any of the steam locomotives depicted! Also No.2002, of which details are unknown. *(L G Marshall)*

50. Sierra Menera: At Sagunto docks 0-6-2T No.201 SAGUNTO, the only Sharp Stewart on the railway, and dating from 1902, is seen at work on 5 April 1961. *(Author)*

51. A superb portrait of one of the Sierra Menera's North British Mallet 0-6-6-0's, No.301 TERUEL. Unfortunately the location and date are unrecorded. *(R T Russell)*

52. On 6 April 1961 the journey up the railway commences, in a four-wheel coach tacked on to the end of this train, hauled by 4-8-0 No.5 YSIDORO, built by North British in 1906. *(Author)*

53. On arrival at Puerto de Escandón the 4-8-0 is replaced by Mallet No.302 PUERTO DE ESCANDON and Garratt No.502. This amount of power will be needed for the return journey with a loaded train, for the climb from Teruel (919m) to Puerto (1,220m). *(Author)*

54. Valencia (CFTV): on 3 June 1953 0-6-0T No.2 (Kerr Stuart 1891) was on shed at Niño Jesus depot. *(Author)*

55. On the same day the 1 p.m. train awaits departure from Villanueva de Castellón behind 4-4-0T No.8 (Hunslet 1904). It is still lettered SVT, a constituent of the CTFV. *(Author)*

56/57. Back at Niño Jesus, shunting is performed by No.101, a steeple cab electric built by MACOSA just two years earlier, in 1951. Also in the station is autovia 102, a six wheel railcar (one powered axle and 4-wheel trailing bogie) built at the adjacent Turia works of the company about 1931. Part of these works can be seen on the left hand side of the photograph. *(Author)*

58. The exterior of Valencia Niño Jesus station as it was in 1953, in the foreground are the tracks of the city tramway system. Totally rebuilt, it is now the control centre of the light rail system. *(Author)*

59. On the other side of the city the terminal station was Puente de Madera where, on 4 June 1953, motor coach No.54 (Devis 1940) and trailers await departure to Liria. *(Author)*

60. On 4 April 1961 a train of the 500 series clerestory stock stands at Valencia Puente de Madera station. This material has an interesting history as it was built by Wumag of Gorlitz in 1927/29, reputedly for a proposed line in northern Portugal which was never constructed, and came to Valencia direct from Germany in 1942/43, presumably overland. Some modifications were required, and one wonders if they had been in store since they were built. *(Author)*

61. All is now changed! Within the last few years modern material has replaced all the older stock. The 3600 series 3-car sets were built by Babcock & Wilcox in 1982.
(E Andres Gramage)

INTRODUCCION

Hace una treintena de años fue publicada la versión original (en inglés) de *'Vapor en la Sierra'* por Peter Allen y Robert Wheeler. Este libro, el cual se ha convertido en una obra clásica, contribuyó a fomentar el interés de los aficionados ingleses por el mundo ferroviario español años antes de la época del turismo en masa de las costas del Mediterráneo. Lamentablemente, esta época comenzó demasiado tarde para salvar algunas preciosas lineas como la de San Feliu de Guixols a Gerona, la cual hoy día sin duda sería considerada como un 'tren turístico', quizás incluso subvencionada por las autoridades regionales.

Es un hecho algo irónico que durante los últimos años hayan sido publicados en España diversos libros sobre los ferrocarriles de vía estrecha, ilustrados en parte por los aficionados ingleses, que eran las únicas personas (había excepciones, por supuesto) que mostraban interés por estas lineas antes de su cierre o modernización. La mayoría de estos libros españoles son estudios en profundidad de lineas sueltas y hasta ahora ha aparecido muy poco sobre el país en su totalidad, salvo las traducciones de varias obras inglesas, incluso *'Vapor en la Sierra'*.

La vía estrecha española ofrecía una enorme diversidad, quizás más amplia que en cualquier otro país europeo durante los años de la posguerra; desde una linea principal, electrificada y de vía métrica, con expresos que incorporaban coches Pullman, hasta largos ferrocarriles rurales, quizás con solamente un 'correo' diario, el cual efectuaba paradas (a veces, paradas muy largas para que los pasajeros pudiesen comer...) en todas las estaciones de su recorrido. Congestionadas redes suburbanas, algunas de las cuales parcialmente electrificadas, servían las conurbaciones como Valencia, Bilbao y Barcelona, mientras que trenes de vapor penetraban por las calles de algunas ciudades como Castellon de la Plana o seguían los caminos rurales de Castilla o Cantabria. En Madrid era posible el transbordo de un tranvía eléctrico urbano a un tren de vapor remolcando un solo coche para la etapa final del recorrido hasta Colmenar Viejo. En Barcelona, iniciando tu viaje en un término subterráneo debajo de una plaza céntrica, llegabas (con tracción eléctrica al principio del recorrido y luego con tracción vapor) al pueblo pirenaico de Guardiola, desde donde era posible seguir hasta Castellar de N'Huch en un tren mixto, de ancho de vía inferior a un metro y ¡gestionado por una fábrica de cementos!

Había un montón de ferrocarriles industriales y mineros en el norte del país. Algunos de estos poseían anchos de vía inusuales; unos pocos habían construido sus propias locomotoras y por la mayoría de estas lineas circulaban trenes para los obreros, ¡en los cuales era posible viajar gratis! Por el contrario, había largas lineas industriales que unían Utrillas con Zaragoza, las minas de Ojos Negros con los altos hornos de Sagunto o Tharsis y Río Tinto con Huelva.

Ahora, la versión inglesa de *'Vapor en la Sierra'* (*'Steam on the Sierra'*) está agotada y los ejemplares de segunda mano se venden a un precio altísimo. Por eso, este libro ofrece un nuevo vistazo a la vía estrecha española de los años cincuenta y sesenta tratando de las lineas de tracción vapor, diesel y eléctrica de un ancho de vía inferior al llamado 'internacional' (así con exclusión de algunas lineas de Barcelona y del FC de Langreo, el último hasta 1984 cuando fue transformado en vía métrica). No trataremos aquí de los ferrocarriles de Mallorca o (con detalle) del FC de Río Tinto, ya que hay libros recientes en inglés sobre sus historias. Excluiremos la mayoría de los tranvías urbanos, aunque hablaremos brevemente de algunas de las redes interurbanas como la de Granada.

Aunque muchos de los ferrocarriles descritos en este libro ya han desaparecido, de ninguna manera está muerta la vía estrecha española - como en el caso de Francia o de Gran Bretaña (aparte de las lineas turísticas). Las redes de vía estrecha española de hoy día consisten en unos 2.000km de lineas 'comerciales', modernizadas y en su mayor parte subvencionadas por el Estado o por las autoridades autónomas; tienen un futuro bastante seguro.

Hoy día es posible recorrer la vía métrica desde Hendaya en Francia hasta Ferrol - más de 800km por las lineas de (ahora) solamente dos empresas, con una mezcla de tracción eléctrica y diesel. El largo FC de La Robla ha perdido sus famosos 'correos', pero dos tramos sobreviven para las mercancías y las cercanías de viajeros; todavía existen algunas lineas industriales. Los ferrocarriles catalanes (algo truncados) y los suburbanos de

Valencia (ahora mejorados, con los dos antiguos sistemas independientes físicamente unidos) son redes florecientes. También prosperan las lineas de montaña de Ribas a Núria (cremallera en parte) y de Cercedilla a Los Cotos (adhesión); en 1990 se hablaba de reconstruir el FC de Montserrat (cremallera) para reducir la congestión en la carretera de acceso al monasterio. Esperamos que algunas ilustraciones recientes, mezcladas con las de la 'nostalgia', sirvan para convencer a los aficionados a la tracción moderna que todavía hay mucho para ofrecerles en España.

La mayoría de las fotos de este libro no han sido publicadas antes en Gran Bretaña, aunque hay excepciones, sobre todo cuando se trata de un asunto de interés excepcional o cuando otras ilustraciones no están disponibles. Algunas han aparecido antes en diversas publicaciones españolas. La bibliografía contiene materiales de referencia donde el lector puede encontrar más información sobre los diversos ferrocarriles o empresas industriales. Esta obra intenta ofrecer algo más que un álbum de fotos sin pretender ser una historia minuciosa y detallada.

Siguiendo los consejos de nuestros numerosos amigos españoles, sin cuya ayuda y hospitalidad durante muchos años habría sido imposible redactar un libro tan detallado, hemos decidido incorporar una versión castellana del texto principal, pensando en aquellos lectores españoles que no entienden muy bien el inglés, pero que tienen ganas de descubrir más acerca de la riqueza de su patrimonio ferroviario de vía estrecha. Agradecemos al Dr. Mike Bent y a la Srta. Estela Ojeda por la traducción.

◻ ◻ ◻ ◻ ◻ ◻ ◻ ◻ ◻

Un poco de información histórica ayudará al lector a comprender los cambios que han tenido lugar en España durante los últimos 25 años. Con pocas excepciones, las fotos más antiguas de este libro son de los años cincuenta, cuando España era un país muy pobre y su industria de turistica no estaba desarrollada. En este época, tenías que conseguir un visado para entrar en el país y el ambiente ferroviario no había cambiado mucho desde los años veinte. La red de vía ancha había sido nacionalizada (RENFE) desde 1941, pero la mayoría de las compañías de vía estrecha eran de carácter independiente, aunque la Jefatura de Explotación de Ferrocarriles por el Estado (EFE) había sido establecida en 1926 para mantener los servicios denominados de utilidad social de las lineas deficitarias. Por eso, había habido muy pocos cierres de los ferrocarriles públicos de vía estrecha hasta los años cincuenta, aunque una o dos lineas habían sido transformadas de vía ancha e incorporadas en la RENFE (por ejemplo, Silla a Cullera en 1935 y Tudela a Tarazona en 1952), mientras que un cierre temprano fue Mollerusa a Balaguer en 1952. Hubo algunos cierres más durante los cincuenta (por ejemplo, 'El Irati' y 'El Plazaola', ambos de Pamplona, y Gerona a Palamós), pero normalmente, si una linea estaba deficitaria, era integrada en la EFE, la cual intentaba rebajar los gastos de explotación y mejorar los servicios a través del uso de automotores y tracción diesel. En 1965 todavía había unos 4.300km de vía estrecha (en contraste con los 5.300km que había a principios de los cincuenta) con un total de 607 locomotoras (sin contar los automotores), 450 de las cuales eran de vapor.

En este último año la EFE se convirtió en FEVE (Ferrocarriles de Vía Estrecha) y a partir de esta fecha la cifra de lineas integradas crecía a medida que las compañías privadas quebraban. Hacia finales de los sesenta muchas lineas habían sido cerradas ya que FEVE, con sus recursos limitados, solamente pudo invertir dinero en los sistemas más rentables. Fue la influencia política lo que consigió en 1972 la terminación de la linea entre Ferrol y Gijón, un proyecto poco rentable. Con la llegada de una administración democrática, algunas autoridades autónomas se hicieron cargo de la redes de vía estrecha dentro de sus territorios (hablamos aquí del País Vasco, Catalunya y Valencia). Hace muchos años, en 1942, la EFE había publicado un proyecto para unir casi todas las redes de vía métrica, a través de la construcción de unos enlaces de poca longitud, pero este plan ambicioso igual que muchos otros no prosperó.

Este estudio de la vía estrecha española comienza en Catalunya y sigue la costa mediterránea hasta la frontera portuguesa; luego vuelve al interior, atravesando Andalucia, para acabar la primera parte de la obra en Granada. En la segunda parte, empezamos en Madrid y pasamos por algunas lineas un poco aisladas en el centro y norte del país antes de comenzar el largísimo recorrido por la costa cantábrica desde la frontera francesa hasta Ferrol. También visitaremos algunos de los ferrocarriles mineros e industriales de esta región, donde la vía métrica verdaderamente es la linea principal y donde la vía ancha solamente alcanza la costa en cinco lugares.

PRIMERA PARTE: DESDE CATALUNYA HASTA LA SIERRA NEVADA

Al cruzar la frontera en Cerbère - Port Bou, el visitante de hoy día descubrirá que la lengua catalana se habla extensamente, incluso para los nombres de los lugares y para los títulos de las empresas. En el texto inglés, el Sr. Rowe ha conservado las versiones castellanas ya que la mayor parte del libro trata de la época franquista y por motivo de coherencia utilizaremos estas formas en el texto castellano.

Primero pararemos en Gerona, una ciudad que tenía tres lineas de vía estrecha, dos de las cuales se acercaban a la costa mientras la tercera penetraba hacia el interior. Aunque la mayoría de las lineas públicas acerca de las cuales hablamos en este libro son o eran de vía métrica, comenzaremos con el FC de San Feliu de Guixols a Gerona, de 750mm. Este ferrocarril, de 40km, fue inaugurado en 1892 y cerrado en 1969; es decir bastante reciente para ser visitado por muchos aficionados ingleses y demasiado pronto para fomentar suficiente interés local para asegurar su supervivencia como una linea turística. Había tracción vapor hasta el cierre y la mayoría de las primeras locomotoras aún existen montadas en pedestales dentro de la región; había seis, de rodaje 0-3-1T, compradas a Krauss entre 1890 y 1905. Durante algunos años circulaban dos 0-4-1T, también procedentes de Krauss; más tarde llegó una locomotora diesel de tres ejes y en 1964 dos 0-3-1T Compound, construidas por Krauss en 1890 y compradas al FC de Onda al Grao de Castellon.

Al otro lado de la linea de RENFE que pasa por Gerona estaba la estación del FC de Olot a Gerona, de vía métrica y de 55km. Esta linea fue construida por una compañía inglesa, pasando bajo gestión española en 1909. La construcción había empezado en Amer en 1895; el tramo hasta Gerona fue inaugurado en 1898, pero hasta 1911 las vías no alcanzaron Olot. Falcon (Loughborough) suministró las primeras locomotoras, de rodaje 0-3-1T; luego, entre 1910 y 1912 llegaron unas 1-3-0T procedentes de St. Leonard (Liège). No obstante, durante la época en que muchos aficionados conocían la linea, la mayoría de los trenes eran remolcados por cuatro 1-3-0T (No. 21 a No. 24), construidas por MTM en 1926.

Como ya hemos dicho, había tres lineas de vía estrecha en Gerona. La primera que fue inaugurada también fue cerrada antes que las otras; se trata del FC de Flassá a Palamós, Gerona y Bañolas (de 750mm) el cual fue construido para facilitar la exportación de corcho a Francia por barcos de cabotaje. El primer tramo, entre Flassá y Palamós, fue inaugurado en 1887; no obstante, la linea no alcanzó Gerona (a 50km de Palamós) hasta 1921 y el ramal de Bañolas (de 14km) fue acabado en 1928. Las primeras locomotoras eran del tipo tranvía y luego llegó un surtido de máquinas procedentes de varios constructores alemanes, la mayoría de ellas de rodaje 0-2-0T o 0-3-0T. Las locomotoras más modernas eran dos 0-3-0T suministradas por Euskalduna en 1928. En este año el ferrocarril experimentó con unos automotores de la casa Krupp-Quintana, pero sin mucho éxito, siendo apartadas las máquinas al año siguiente. Sucedió lo mismo con unos automotores de construcción artesanal en 1931. Así, la tracción vapor dominaba hasta el cierre de la linea en 1956. El trazado era caracterizado por sus fuertes rampas y había varios tramos que seguían las carreteras. El autor tuvo suerte en recorrer la linea durante su primera visita a España en 1953.

Antes de abandonar Gerona, echamos un vistazo a los servicios que ofrecían estos ferrocarriles en 1954 y 1965. En 1954 había cinco trenes diarios a Olot; los más rápidos tardaban un poco más de dos horas, omitiendo tres o cuatro paradas, mientras que los 'mixtos' tardaban más de dos horas y media con 16 paradas. Solo cuatro trenes regresaban hasta Gerona (dos 'rápidos' y dos 'mixtos') y según las notas en el 'Horario Guía' enlazaban allí con "la linea del MZA"... Para 1965 habían llegado los automotores, que realizaron el recorrido en 90 minutos, efectuando algunos servicios de cercanías los días de los mercados. El horario, aunque más complicado que en 1954, estaba probablemente más estrechamente regulado a las necesidades de las comunidades locales. En la linea de Sant Feliu, en 1954 había cinco trenes diarios, los cuales tardaban alrededor de dos horas, y la situación cambiaría muy poco diez años más tarde. En la linea de Palamós el tren directo más rápido tardaba 140 minutos en recorrer 50km; había dos circulaciones diarias en cada sentido. En el ramal de Bañolas había tres trenes directos y éstos tardaban 50 minutos en recorrer 16km.

En 1953 Barcelona ofreció casi todo lo que deseaba un aficionado a los transportes públicos. Había una red de tranvías y un metro, ambos con redes de dos anchos de vía, tres funiculares, una acera móvil (más antigua

62. Carcagente - Denia: Most frequently seen in action in the later years were the Belgian built 060T's. On 7 October 1967 No.24 was to be seen working the 8.55 a.m. from Carcagente to Denia at Tabernes.
(L G Marshall)

63. On 17 June 1961 No.21, the first of the batch, is to be found at Gandia station on a goods train.
(D W Winkworth)

64. The earliest locomotives on the line were Black Hawthorn 4-4-0ST's, and here the first of them, No.1 of 1881, is carriage shunting at Carcagente in 1961. *(D W Winkworth)*

65. The line also had two 'Wismar' double ended railcars, a number of which were built under licence by Carde y Escoriaza of Zaragoza in 1933/34 and 1936. Both broad and narrow gauge examples were built, and five went to the Norte for their Tudela - Tarazona and Carcagente - Denia metre gauge lines. WMG4, seen here in 1965 at Carcagente, was delivered here in 1934, together with WMG3, which went to Amorbieta - Bermeo in 1967, while No.4 was scrapped. Only one narrow gauge example survives today, ex Madrid - Aragon, in very much rebuilt condition. *(Author)*

que la de la estación de Bank, de Londres, y la primera que el autor había visto) y un teleférico que cruzaba el puerto hasta Montjuich. Durante los cincuenta éste último no funcionaba, pero más tarde fue restaurado. Había trolebuses, autobuses de dos pisos y ferrocarriles de tres anchos de vía. La red de vía métrica más extensa de Catalunya siempre ha sido la de la Compañía General de los FFCC Catalanes (CGFC), que fue formada por la fusión de diversas compañías pequeñas. A partir de 1926 había servicios de cercanías (manejados durante 30 años por solamente cuatro locomotoras) en los primeros 11km de la linea principal, los cuales habían sido electrificados con 1500V. Desde su término debajo de la Plaza de España, la linea principal penetraba las estribaciones de los Pirineos hasta Guardiola, a 132km de Barcelona. Había varios ramales, algunos de estos de carácter industrial, y un transporte intensivo de carbón desde el interior hasta el puerto de Barcelona. Una curiosidad de esta linea era que ya que la concesión para el tramo de Manresa a Olvan caducó antes de las de los otros tramos, esta parte de la linea era gestionada por la EFE con locomotoras que llevaban las letras 'M–O', situadas en el depósito de Sallent. Aunque había coches directos entre Barcelona y Guardiola, cambiaban las locomotoras en Manresa y Olvan. El parque de vapor era diverso: desde unas pequeñas 0-3-0T compradas a MTM, a través de un grupo de 1-3-0T y 1-3-1T de origen belga (cuatro de las 1-3-1T fueron construidas en 1948), hasta ocho máquinas Garratt suministradas por St. Leonard durante los años veinte. Cuatro de las Garratt circulaban en el tramo gestionado por la EFE, donde también era posible observar cuatro 1-2-2-0T procedentes de los FFCC Réticos de Suiza. Las primeras locomotoras diesel llegaron a mediados de los cincuenta.

A causa de la disminución del tráfico, la linea principal al norte de Manresa fue cerrada en 1973. FEVE se hizo cargo de la red de la CGFC en 1976; tres años más tarde el sistema pasó a la Generalitat de Catalunya. A partir de los sesenta, la catenaria fue prolongada; hasta Martorell en 1968, a Monistrol en 1971, alcanzando Manresa (a 63km de Barcelona) en 1984. El ramal de 37km de Martorell a Igualada (transporte de viajeros) sigue con tracción diesel, así como los ramales de mercancías de Manresa a Súria (13km) y a Sallent (7,5km). Recientemente ha sido construido un nuevo acceso de 12km al puerto de Barcelona. Hoy día los transportes más importantes de mercancías son sales potasicas. Los trenes son remolcados por unas locomotoras diesel Bo Bo compradas a Alsthom durante los cincuenta y tres Co Co suministradas por MACOSA en 1990. Durante los ochenta las unidades diesel de la linea de Igualada fueron remozadas, mientras que nuevas unidades eléctricas aparecieron en la linea de Manresa. En el depósito de Martorell-Enllaç hay tres máquinas antiguas conservadas en estado de funcionamiento: una de las eléctricas de 1926, una 0-3-0T (No. 31) y una 1-3-1T (OLOT No. 22), esta última procedente del FC de Gerona a Olot. De vez en cuando salen por las lineas principales para remolcar trenes especiales. Otras locomotoras de la CGFC han sido montadas en pedestales dentro de la región.

Entre Barcelona y Guardiola la CGFC enlazaba con otros dos ferrocarriles; el primero de estos era la linea de cremallera de Montserrat. Pertenecía a la Sociedad de Ferrocarriles de Montaña a Grandes Pendientes (FMGP), la cual también gestionaba el ferrocarril de cremallera de Ribes a Núria. Los 8,5km de vía métrica entre Monistrol (Norte) y Montserrat fueron inaugurados por tramos entre 1892 y 1905 y Cail suministró cinco 0-2-1T. Entre 1921 y 1923 llegaron tres 0-2-1T más; dos de nueva construcción y una de segunda mano comprada al FC de Gornergrat de Suiza. Todas fueron productos de SLM. A partir de 1947 el ferrocarril se deficitó. Después de un accidente funesto en 1953, la FMGP estudió la modernización del sistema, pero a pesar de ello la linea fue cerrada en 1957. Las locomotoras se quedaron en su depósito durante muchos años después del cierre, y recientemente algunas han sido restauradas por fuera para servir como 'monumentos' locales. En la estación de Monistrol de FGC se puede ver una de estas máquinas con dos coches de viajeros, cuya restauración ha sido subvencionada por la Asociación Automovilista de Catalunya.

En 1955 el autor viajó a Guardiola y se asombraba encontrar en la calle delante de la estación unas vías de 600mm y un tren a punto de salir. Antes, él creía que este ferrocarril, que apareció en el horario, era una extensión de vía métrica de la red de los Catalanes. Con una longitud de 12km, era gestionado por Cementos Asland y los pasajeros viajaban en un coche en la cola de los trenes largos y empolvados de vagones de cemento. La linea había sido inaugurada en 1908, en presencia de Alfonso XIII, pero los servicios públicos entre Guardiola y La Pobla de Lillet no comenzaron hasta 1914, siendo acabada la extensión de 2km hasta Castellar de N'Huch en 1924. La linea, que seguía la carretera, era manejada por unas O & K 0-2-0T. Cuando se cerró en 1963 fue el último de los ferrocarriles españoles de 600mm con un servicio público de viajeros. Un grupo de aficionados catalanes ha establecido una colección de material móvil en Castellar de N'Huch, con la espera de ubicar un museo ferroviario y de la arqueología industrial.

Para el aficionado que llega a España por la linea de Tolosa (Francia) y la estación de frontera de La Tour de Carol, la primera parada obligatoria es en Ribes de Freser, para recorrer la linea de vía métrica de Núria, que tiene tramos de adhesión y de cremallera. Fue construida por la FMGP, electrificad a con 1500V e inaugurada en 1931. Durante su construcción fueron empleadas dos de las máquinas de la linea de Montserrat, una de las cuales ahora está conservada en el depósito de Ribes-Vila. El ferrocarril tiene 12,5km de largo y el tramo de cremallera es del sistema ABT. Núria, a una altura de 1.965m, es la estación de ferrocarril más alta de España. Las cuatro locomotoras originales, de tres ejes, son de construcción suiza, mientras que los coches fueron comprados a una empresa alemana. Había pocos cambios en la linea hasta los años ochenta cuando la Generalitat de Catalunya compró un 70 por ciento de las acciones de la compañía, siendo integrada la linea en los Ferrocarriles de la Generalitat de Catalunya (FGC) en 1986. Para absorber el creciente tráfico de ocio (el esquí en invierno, el montañismo en verano), fueron construidos tres nuevos automotores en Barcelona bajo licencia suiza en 1986, mientras que los coches de viajeros junto con tres de las cuatro locomotoras originales de 1931 fueron remozados. En 1992 un automotor más fue encargado. La linea de Núria es ahora el único ferrocarril de cremallera de España y su futuro parece asegurado.

Después de haber regresado a Barcelona, seguimos la costa por Tarragona hasta Salou. El FC Económico de Reus a Salou, una linea de 8km, fue inaugurado en 1887. Falcon suministró todas sus locomotoras; las tres primeras del tipo 'tranvía' y las otras de rodaje 0-2-0T. Algunos vagones de mercancías y 28 coches de viajeros fueron también comprados a Falcon. En 1926 la compañía construyó en sus propios talleres cinco coches más, uno de los cuales fue transformado al año siguiente en un automotor térmico. En 1932 llegó una 0-3-1T (construida por Falcon - Brush Engineering en 1899), procedente del FC de Olot a Gerona. Durante la Guerra Civil algunos de los coches y una de las locomotoras tipo 'tranvía' fueron destrozados. Después, la compañía tuvo poco éxito en su búsqueda de material de viajeros de segunda mano. Algunos coches fueron comprados a las lineas de Mollerusa a Balaguer, Monistrol a Montserrat y Madrid a Almorox, pero fueron revendidos o desguazados poco después. Dos automotores Billard aparecieron en 1958, seguidos por un automotor Ferrotrade en 1966; este último tuvo poco éxito. No obstante, a pesar de la competencia de las carreteras, el ferrocarril, todavía en manos privadas, sobrevivió hasta 1970 cuando fue comprado por una empresa de transporte de carretera, que lo cerró cinco años después. Las tres 0-2-0T han sido conservadas en pedestales en la comarca.

Abandonamos Catalunya y entramos en la comunidad autónoma valenciana, una región de arroz y de naranjas, desde donde proceden los vagones de TRANSFESA los cuales reparten la fruta por todas partes de Europa. Encontramos la primera red de vía estrecha en Castellon de la Plana, donde el FC de Onda al Grao de Castellon (de 750mm) penetraba las calles urbanas de los pueblos de su recorrido. La linea principal, que tenía una longitud de 28,5km, comenzaba en el puerto de Grao, pasaba por la ciudad de Castellon de la Plana y terminaba en Onda; fue inaugurada por tramos entre 1888 y 1890. Había un ramal entre Vila-Real y Burriana (de 10,5km) inaugurado en 1907. El parque de vapor consistía en varias 0-3-0T y 0-3-1T compradas a Krauss entre 1888 y 1890; las 0-3-1T eran del tipo Compound. Los coches eran de dos ejes, con balconcillos y de construcción nacional. En 1927 llegaron unos automotores térmicos, que no tuvieron mucho éxito, siendo transformados más tarde en coches de viajeros. Sus remolques, junto con dos de las 0-3-1T Compound, fueron vendidos al FC de San Feliu a Gerona y en cambio, procedentes de la linea de Gerona a Palamós, llegaron algunos coches tipo bogie y las dos 0-3-0T construidas por Euskalduna. En 1931 la linea fue incorporada en la EFE. Las perdidas siguieron aumentando a medida que crecía la competencia de la carretera, causando el abandono de un proyecto para electrificar la red. Había placas giratorias (cosa poco usual en tales lineas) en Grao y en Onda, mientras que los talleres muy bien dotados de Grao también reparaban las locomotoras enviadas allí por las otras compañías de vía estrecha del sureste de España, incluso las máquinas del FC de Cartagena a Los Blancos, de un ancho de vía de 1067mm. Creemos que las 0-3-0T de Gerona, aunque fueron remozadas, nunca entraron en servicio. La red fue cerrada en 1963.

66. ESA, Alicante: 2-6-0T No.5 waiting to leave Denia for Alicante. This locomotive is the first of six built by MTM in 1913. Four others were built by Hanomag in the same year and despite its number this one carries a Hanomag plate! *(late N W Newcombe, Author's collection)*

67. A panorama of Alicante (Marina) station, with another 2-6-0T, No.7, travelling towards Denia, on 25 April 1957. *(J Wiseman)*

68. By 1993 Alicante has developed into a leading tourist resort, and high rise apartments are in evidence behind the 'Limon Express' tourist train. However the station building survives, though the canopy is not original, and the whole picture is overseen by the Castle of Santa Barbara, which was no doubt in situ long before anything in the foreground! *(J Orts)*

Ahora llegamos al primer ferrocarril de carácter puramente industrial que figura en este libro. Se trata de la red de vía métrica, con tracción vapor y eléctrica, del complejo de los Altos Hornos de Vizcaya en Sagunto. El parque de vapor era muy diverso, con unas máquinas de segunda mano procedentes del FC de Alcoy a Gandía (dos 1-3-1T), de los FFCC Vascongados (una 2-2-0T), de los Réticos (una 1-3-1T), del FC de Santander a Bilbao (tres 2-2-0T construidas por Dübs) y de la SVT de Valencia. Con la excepción de dos, todas las locomotoras databan del siglo XIX; la más moderna había sido construida por los AHV en su complejo de Bilbao en 1941. Afortunadamente, los visitantes a los AHV fueron bienvenidos y les ofrecieron visitas guiadas.

Si el complejo siderúrgico era de interés, en mayor grado era la manera de suministrarlo con el mineral de hierro. Entre Sagunto y las minas de Ojos Negros había un ferrocarril de vía métrica y de 204km, propiedad de la Compañía Minera de Sierra Menera. Durante la mayor parte de su recorrido, la linea seguía la de RENFE (de Zaragoza a Valencia por Teruel) y en el Puerto de Escandón alcanzó una altura de más de 1000m; por eso necesitaba unas locomotoras potentes. Cuando fue inaugurada en 1907 North British suministró 14 2-4-0T; dos máquinas más del mismo tipo siguieron en 1913. North British también construyó cuatro 0-3-3-0 tipo Mallet y Euskalduna suministró dos locomotoras Garratt. Para maniobras en Sagunto y en las minas había un parque reducido de locomotoras de rodaje 0-3-0T y 0-3-2T e incluso algunas pequeñas locomotoras diesel. Entre 1964 y 1966 llegaron cinco locomotoras diesel hidráulicas, construidas por Henschel, para remolcar trenes en la linea principal. No obstante, un cambio de la estructura tarifaria de RENFE produjo el cierre de la linea de vía métrica (cuya operación debe haber sido muy costosa) en 1972 y la construcción de un ramal de vía ancha hasta las minas. Las locomotoras diesel fueron vendidas a FEVE. A principios de siglo, el FC Central de Aragón había resistido la construcción de la otra linea, pero cuando casi 70 años más tarde su sucesora (la RENFE) consiguió el tráfico del mineral, su triunfo fue breve, ya que una recesión de la industria siderúrgica unida con la importación creciente de mineral barato desde el extranjero produjeron una bajada de actividad en el complejo de Sagunto. Las minas de Ojos Negros, aunque no agotadas, se encontraron con problemas económicos y la compañía entró en liquidación en 1987. Un viaje por este ferrocarril era una experiencia memorable, con doble tracción de las locomotoras Mallet o Garratt a través del Puerto de Escandón.

Volvemos a la costa. En Valencia había tres compañías distintas, las cuales construyeron lineas suburbanas de vía métrica. El primer tramo de la linea de Valencia (Jesús) a Vila Nova de Castelló fue inaugurado en 1893, siendo alcanzado este último pueblo (a 52,5km de Valencia) en 1915. Al norte de la ciudad la SVT construyó lineas hasta Lliria, Bétera y Rafelbuñol entre 1888 y 1893, mientras que entre Valencia y El Grao había un tranvía de vapor cuyo recorrido de 6km fue electrificado en 1900.

En 1911 la SVT, que por estas fechas se había hecho cargo de la linea de El Grao, tenía su sede en Francia. Las lineas pasaron a gestión nacional con la fundación en 1917 de la Compañía de Tranvías y Ferrocarriles de Valencia (CTFV), que en 1946 se hizo cargo del ferrocarril de Vila Nova. Durante los años veinte había comenzado la electrificación de la red al norte de la ciudad, cuando el parque de vapor consistía en unas 2-2-0T y 0-3-0T construidas por Hunslet. Algunas de estas máquinas fueron vendidas a la compañía de Vila Nova, cuyas primeras locomotoras eran unas 0-3-0T suministradas por Kerr Stuart y por Avonside. Esta linea también tenía algunos automotores térmicos y más tarde, unas pocas locomotoras eléctricas para maniobras. La red entera de la CTFV se quedó electrificada en 1955, siendo desguazadas durante esta época la mayoría de las locomotoras de vapor.

En 1964 la EFE se hizo cargo de la red de la CTFV. Bajo su gestión, el sistema fue decayendo cada vez más siendo rescatado al final por el gobierno autónomo, el cual fundó los Ferrocarriles de la Generalitat Valenciana en 1988. Hace poco hubo grandes inversiones para unir las dos redes, al norte y al sur de la ciudad por un túnel, formando así un moderno metro. El túnel fue inaugurado en octubre de 1988, cuando fueron nombradas cuatro lineas de servicios: (1) de Bétera a Vila Nova, (2) de Lliria a Torrent, (3) de Pont de Fusta a Rafelbuñol y (4) de Ademuz a Grao por Pont de Fusta. Desafortunadamente, la red todavía no está completamente integrada, ya que las antiguas compañías utilizaban corrientes de 600V y 650V y durante los ochenta todas las lineas salvo las de Rafelbuñol y de Grao fueron transformadas a 1500V. A finales de 1990 la linea de Ademuz a Grao fue cerrada para ser transformada en un tranvía moderno de 9km con 37 paradas y con una corriente de 750V. Recientemente, cuatro unidades del tipo 'metro ligero' con suelo bajo han sido suministradas por

Siemens Duewag y se prevee que la linea será reinaugurada durante la segunda mitad de 1994. La linea de Rafelbuñol va a ser prolongada por debajo de la ciudad hasta un nuevo término más céntrico; también hay un proyecto para otra linea de metro denominada 'Linea 5'. Las antiguas unidades eléctricas, algunas procedentes de los FFCC Vicinal de Bélgica, han sido apartadas y entre 1986 y 1990 fueron entregadas cuarenta unidades articuladas de construcción nacional. También hay diez unidades construidas por Babcock y Wilcox en 1981, mientras que en la linea de 650V de Rafelbuñol todavía circulan algunas unidades antiguas, construidas en 1952 pero remozadas entre 1982 y 1989.

El viajero de los años cincuenta podía salir de la estación de RENFE de Valencia a bordo de un tren de cercanías de dos pisos. Por supuesto, ¡los coches no tenían nada en común con los modernos vehículos de dos pisos que entraron en servicio en las cercanías de Madrid en 1990! En Carcagente la linea de RENFE enlazaba con la de vía métrica que iba hasta Denia; esta linea también enlazaba con las de tres compañías más y casi formaba una ruta de vía métrica entre Valencia y Alicante.

Inaugurada entre Carcagente y Gandía en 1864 con tracción de sangre (¡35,5km en 3 horas!), esta fue la primera linea de vía métrica en España. Fue prolongada hasta Denia (a 65,5km de Carcagente) en 1884; por esta fecha, por supuesto ¡el tipo de tracción había cambiado! Se dice que hasta principios de este siglo fueron utilizados unos coches de dos ejes y de dos pisos en los trenes de viajeros. El propietario original de la linea era el FC de Almansa a Valencia y Tarragona; luego pasó a manos del Norte y la EFE se hizo cargo de ella en 1942. Black Hawthorn suministró las primeras locomotoras, unas 2-2-0T, seguidas de un grupo de máquinas de procedencia belga de rodaje 0-3-0T. Más tarde, dos locomotoras fueron compradas a la linea vecina, de Silla a Cullera, cuando esta última fue transformada en vía ancha en 1935. Hasta la llegada de un parque de automotores (del tipo de serie encargado por cuenta de la EFE) en 1958, había también dos antiguos automotores térmicos de dos testeros. En 1959 fue inaugurado un nuevo servicio directo entre Carcagente y Alicante, por las vías del FC de Alicante a Denia (por aquellas fechas también una parte de la EFE); un recorrido de 160km en 3 horas y 40 minutos. A pesar de estas mejoras el tramo entre Carcagente y Gandía fue cerrado en 1969, siendo luego incorporada una parte del trazado en la extensión de la linea de RENFE desde Cullera hasta Gandía, inaugurada en 1972. La vía métrica entonces consistía en una linea de 124km, pasando por las urbanizaciones en desarrollo de la Costa Blanca. Curiosamente, a pesar del turismo creciente de la región, el tramo entre Gandía y Denia fue cerrado en 1974.

La Compañía de los Ferrocarriles Estratégicos y Secundarios de Alicante (ESA) construyó la linea entre Alicante y Denia; fue inaugurada por tramos entre 1914 y 1915 y tiene 93,5km de longitud. Su parque de vapor consistía en unas 1-3-0T construidas por HANOMAG y MTM en 1913. Los primeros automotores con remolques, de construcción artesanal en los talleres del ferrocarril, aparecieron en 1949/50 seguidos por unos automotores Billard en 1958. Desde 1988 la linea ha sido gestionada por FGV. Hay trenes frecuentes, sobre todo entre Alicante y Benidorm, desde donde circula el tren turístico denominado el 'Limón Exprés'. Los coches de este tren procedían de las lineas de Manresa a Olvan y de Carcagente a Denia y fueron remozados por un taller artesanal de Alcoy en 1987. Es una lástima que el 'Limón Exprés' no circule con tracción vapor. En 1992 la linea tenía dos locomotoras diesel hidráulicas construidas por Babcock y Wilcox bajo licencia Alsthom en 1959 y dos más, de rodaje 0-3-0, construidas por Batignolles-Besain sobre la misma fecha. Los automotores corrientes consisten en ocho unidades construidas por MAN en 1967 y remozadas en 1984.

Ahora regresamos hasta Gandía, donde el FC de Carcagente a Gandía enlazaba con el FC de Alcoy al Puerto de Gandía, una linea de 53km construida por una compañía inglesa en 1893. Hasta su cierre en 1969, todos sus trenes eran remolcados por ocho 1-3-1T construidas por Beyer Peacock en 1890/91; dos fueron vendidas al complejo de los AHV de Sagunto en 1947. Al principio también había una 0-3-0T, un producto de Manning Wardle, que probablemente fue utilizada durante la construcción de la linea y vendida a la linea de Alcoy a Yecla en 1920. En Gandía las dos lineas de vía métrica se cruzaban al nivel, pero aunque había un enlace físico, las dos compañías conservaban sus propias estaciones. A partir de 1963 la linea de Alcoy fue gestionada por la EFE, pero a diferencia de las lineas de la costa, evitó la modernización. Una de las locomotoras, la No. 7, ha sido conservada como monumento cerca de la nueva estación de RENFE de Gandía.

69. Cartagena - Los Blancos: No.4 TITAN (Hunslet 1883) at Santa Lucia depot, 10 April 1956.
(Author)

70. Alcoy - Gandía: right up to its sad demise in 1969, this line presented a perfect 'time capsule' of a British equipped light railway, operated in a Mediterranean setting. On 1 October 1963 2-6-2T No.2 VILLALONGA (Beyer Peacock 1890) shunts passenger stock at Gandía. *(Author)*

71. On 29 March 1965 No.5 GAYANES is ready to leave Alcoy with the 5.25 p.m. to Gandía.
(Author)

72. En route the train passes beneath the ruined castle at Lorcha, a timeless scene that can have changed little since 1890. The coach was built in Manchester in that year and the locomotive is of the same vintage.
(Author)

En la estación de empalme de Muro de Alcoy comenzaba la larga linea (102km) de los Ferrocarriles Económicos de Villena a Alcoy y Yecla (VAY). Los trenes del VAY siempre terminaban su recorrido en la estación de Alcoy del FC de Alcoy al Puerto de Gandía, a 10km de Muro de Alcoy. El VAY fue inaugurado por tramos entre 1884 y 1909 y luego se hizo cargo del FC de Jumilla a Cieza, de 32km, inaugurado en 1921. Había un parque de vapor de procedencia alemana, la mayoría de las máquinas de rodaje 0-3-0T, aunque también había dos productos de Couillet; todas databan de 1883. Para la linea de Jumilla a Cieza, Vulcan suministró dos 1-3-1T y fue comprada la Manning Wardle del FC de Alcoy al Puerto de Gandía. Los primeros automotores llegaron en 1931 y, su capacidad aumentada por el uso de unos antiguos remolques de dos ejes, poco a poco tomaban la mayor parte del transporte de viajeros. La linea, incorporada en FEVE en 1965, fue cerrada en 1969. De los 348km de vía métrica integrada que solían servir a las provincias de Murcia, Valencia y Alicante, solo quedan los 94 de la linea de Alicante a Denia.

¡Ahora cambiamos de ancho de vía! El FC de Cartagena a La Unión y Los Blancos, que solía tener un ancho de 1067mm, era gestionado al principio por una empresa inglesa que se llamaba Cartagena and Herrerías Steam Tramways Co. Ltd. El primer tramo fue inaugurado en 1874 y las vías alcanzaron Los Blancos en 1897, pero bajo la dirección de una compañía belga. A causa de la recesión de la industria minera durante los años veinte, la linea se encontró en dificultades, siendo incorporada en la EFE en 1931. Había un parque de vapor bastante extenso; unas 0-2-0ST, 0-3-0ST y 0-3-0T construidas por Hunslet y Manning Wardle y seis locomotoras Sentinel, de caldera vertical, las cuales sobrevivieron, aunque apartadas, hasta los sesenta. En 1960 llegaron una locomotora diesel hidráulica y dos automotores Billard. Durante 1972/73 el ancho de vía fue convertido en métrico y en 1976 un nuevo tramo entre El Estrecho y Los Nietos (a 19km de Cartagena) fue inaugurado, siendo abandonado el trazado original entre El Estrecho y Los Blancos. Hoy día circulan unidades MAN de FEVE, y el único transporte es de viajeros.

Tenemos un recorrido muy largo, pero muy paisajístico hasta el próximo lugar de interés del punto de vista de la vía estrecha, es decir, la ciudad de Málaga. La Compañía de los Ferrocarriles Suburbanos de Málaga (FSM) tenía tres lineas de vía métrica. Hacia el este salía la linea de Vélez-Málaga (de 36km) inaugurada en 1908. Desde allí la linea fue prolongada hasta Ventas de Zafarraya, a 68km de la ciudad; este tramo, que incorporaba una cremallera para superar las montañas, fue inaugurado en 1922. Hacia el suroeste salía la linea de Coín (de 40km) acabada en 1913. Antes de 1934 el servicio entre Málaga y Fuengirola (30km) había sido gestionado por los FSM, pero luego el ramal de San Julián a Fuengirola fue incorporado en la EFE, cuyos trenes tenían que recorrer 8km de las vías de los FSM para alcanzar la ciudad. La mayor parte del parque de vapor de los FSM consistía en unas 0-3-0T construidas por Tubize en 1906 y las locomotoras de cremallera fueron suministradas por SLM entre 1920 y 1924. La EFE trajo tres 0-3-0T construidas por Falcon en 1887/88 para el FC Vasco-Navarro, el cual recientemente había sido electrificado. Más tarde llegaron tres 0-3-0T, suministradas en 1886 por Couillet al FC de Tudela a Tarazona, el cual fue convertido en vía ancha en 1952. Como una parte de su plan de modernización de 1958/59 la EFE consiguió algunos automotores para la linea de Fuengirola. A partir de estas fechas, la llamada 'Costa del Sol' estaba en pleno desarrollo y esta linea fue transformada en vía ancha y electrificada entre 1971 y 1975; ahora es una parte de la RENFE y tiene un servicio intensivo de viajeros. Lamentablemente el resto de la red de los FSM ha desaparecido.

Seguimos hasta Sevilla, donde en las afueras de la ciudad dos ferrocarriles de vía métrica bajaban desde el interior hasta los muelles del río Guadalquivir. La más larga de estas lineas (97km) subía hasta las Minas de Cala y tenía diversos ramales, uno de los cuales casi alcanzaba la red del FC de Río Tinto. Hasta 1938 había trenes de viajeros, pero veinte años más tarde la linea estaba prácticamente cerrada. Por aquellas fechas era posible alcanzar el depósito, ubicado en San Juan de Aznalfarache, cerca del río, mediante el tranvía eléctrico desde Sevilla.

El FC de Aznalcóllar al Guadalquivir, cuyo depósito estaba en Camas (otra parada en la red de tranvías urbanos), tenía unos 48km de vías, pero durante los años cincuenta solo había circulaciones regulares (¡locomotoras de vía métrica remolcando vagones de vía ancha!) en el tramo entre Camas (donde había un enlace con la linea de las Minas de Cala) y el río. Para la linea de las Minas de Cala Borsig suministró unas 0-2-0T y 0-3-2T pero a medida que el tráfico disminuía algunas fueron vendidas a otros ferrocarriles. La linea de Aznalcóllar tenía un parque de máquinas compradas a Jung y a Krauss con rodaje 0-3-1T. En ambas lineas las locomotoras tenían nombres.

Desde Sevilla nos dirigimos hacia la frontera portuguesa. En la linea de Huelva está la estación de La Palma del Condado, desde donde salía un ferrocarril hasta Bollullos del Condado. Funcionaba entre 1921 y 1931 y era una linea de viajeros, con un ancho de vía de 600mm. Su parque de vapor era de interés especial, ya que consistía en dos 2-3-0T, ALMONTE y BOLLULLOS, construidas por Hunslet en 1918 para el War Department (Ministerio de la Guerra) británico. También había una locomotora de gasolina de 40CV construida por Motor Rail - Simplex para el War Department. A causa de una avería de la BOLLULLOS (las otras dos máquinas ya habían sido apartadas) el 8 de noviembre de 1931 la linea fue cerrada. Curiosamente, la linea figuraba todavía en el 'Horario Guía' de 1954, pero con la nota "no presta servicio de viajeros".

En Las Mallas, todavía en la linea de Huelva, las vías de 1067mm del FC de Río Tinto pasan por debajo de las de 1674mm y los dos ferrocarriles siguen juntos hasta la ciudad. De todos los ferrocarriles industriales españoles el de Río Tinto es probablemente el más conocido. Su linea principal, de 83km, fue inaugurada en 1875; tenía más locomotoras que cualquier otro ferrocarril de vía estrecha en España. Aparte de unos productos de Baldwin, los cuales fueron desguazados durante los años treinta, su parque de vapor reflejaba los orígines ingleses de la compañía minera. Había un montón de máquinas de rodaje 0-3-0T, dos locomotoras Garratt, un grupo de locomotoras ténder de rodaje 1-3-0 construidas en 1953 (las cuales remolcaban la mayoría de los trenes de la linea principal a partir de aquella fecha) y una deliciosa 0-2-0T con grua, esta última construida por Hawthorn Leslie. Pero para conocer más acerca de esta encantadora linea dirigimos al lector al libro publicado por Plateway Press en 1991.

Antes de llegar a Huelva pasamos por el pueblo de San Juan del Puerto, desde donde una linea de 1067mm subía hasta Valverde, Buitrón y Zalamea. Inaugurada en 1868, era al principio la propiedad de la United Alkali Co. (inglesa), la cual fue uno de los constitutivos de la ICI. Había un servicio de viajeros entre 1874 y 1934, pero a medida que se agotaban las minas disminuía el tráfico y en 1942 la linea fue incorporada en la EFE, la cual restableció el servicio de viajeros. Según el 'Horario Guía' de 1954 había tres trenes diarios entre San Juan y Buitrón, una distancia de 36km, y un tren mixto entre Valverde y Zalamea, un recorrido de 21km. Había un enlace en Zalamea con los trenes del FC de Río Tinto con destino a Nerva. En 1965 había un servicio de automotores entre San Juan y Zalamea, pero este tuvo poco éxito y tres años más tarde la linea cerró. El parque de vapor consistía en unas 0-3-0T y 2-3-0T construidas por Kitson y dos 2-3-0T suministradas por Andrew Barclay; todas tenían nombres y la más moderna databa de 1908.

Ahora vamos a visitar un ferrocarril que, después del Río Tinto, fue probablemente el más conocido de las lineas mineras de esta región; se trata del FC de Tharsis. La concesión fue otorgada en 1866 a la Tharsis Copper and Sulphur Company, la cual amplió el puerto de Puntal de la Cruz en la orilla derecha del Odiel, enfrente de la ciudad de Huelva. Aunque poco conocida por los turistas, Huelva es una ciudad conocidísima entre los aficionados al ferrocarril industrial. Deberíamos recordar que la riqueza minera de las sierras del interior de la provincia lleva más de mil años siendo explotada, y que Colón embarcó del puerto vecino de Palos para descubrir el Nuevo Mundo. El ancho de vía de la linea de Tharsis es de 1219mm (cuatro pies) el mismo que en el metro de Glasgow, la ciudad donde la empresa minera tenía su sede. La linea principal entre Tharsis y Puntal es de 46km y había un servicio de viajeros … ¡un tren en cada sentido, los lunes! El parque de vapor consistía en unas 1-4-0T construidas por Hohenzollern entre 1923 y 1929 y diversas 1-4-0T y 0-4-0T suministradas por North British entre 1930 y 1935; todas tenían nombres. En las minas de Tharsis y de La Zarza había también algunas locomotoras diesel. Las primeras máquinas eran unas 0-2-0T y 0-3-0T compradas a Dübs, de las cuales la No. 1 ODIEL de 1867 ha sobrevivido. Ahora hay tracción diesel - unas máquinas Bo Bo construidas en Francia en 1966 - pero la linea no tiene un futuro muy asegurado y se habla de su cierre durante 1994 a causa de los problemas de la empresa minera.

Después de haber seguido la costa desde la frontera francesa hasta la de Portugal, echaremos un breve vistazo a la zona minera de las sierras al norte de Huelva, donde había varias lineas de vía estrecha, la mayoría de ellas con un ancho de vía de 762mm.

73. VAY: this photograph appears at first to be of a freight train in action, but on 27 May 1969 the railway had closed and it is in fact a rake of wagons which has been gathered up at Villena by No.5 (Hartmann 1883) and brought in for burning, an act that was carried out forthwith. *(L G Marshall)*

74. Personally, I never saw a steam locomotive on this railway, though I travelled the length of it. On 29 March 1965 at Villena was 70 hp 4-wheel diesel railcar No.2, a smart little vehicle but capable of giving a very rough ride at speed. *(Author)*

75/76. Málaga suburban: Two views of the Málaga to Coín train on 18 April 1962. The locomotive is No.28 (Tubize 1906) and it is seen arriving at Churriana where some planks are being handled. Note the condition of the train and of the track, especially in the station. *(Author)*

A principios de los años sesenta ya había cerrado el ferrocarril de 762mm de la Compañía Española de Explosivos de Sotiel Coronado. No obstante, todavía quedaba por fotografiar una 0-2-0T abandonada construida por Barclay. Esta linea había sido de origen inglés.La linea de 762mm de la Société Française des Pyrites de Huelva llevaba el mineral desde las minas de San Telmo hasta la estación de RENFE de Valdelamusa, donde había transbordo para la bajada en vagones de vía ancha hasta Huelva. Durante los sesenta había tracción diesel, siendo apartadas las antiguas 0-2-0T y 0-3-0T de procedencia alemana.

Al otro lado de las vías de RENFE en Valdelamusa había un ferrocarril de 10km y de 630mm de origen inglés, el cual iba a las minas de Cuevas de la Mora. Según las fuentes de documentación, una de sus locomotoras era una 0-2-0T, ROSALIA, suministrada por Kerr Stuart en 1902. Cuando el autor estuvo en Valdelamusa en 1964, no quedaba el menor vestigio de esta linea.

El FC de Minas de San Miguel, de 18km y de 600mm, también enlazaba con el de RENFE entre Huelva y Zafra. Tenía dos 0-3-0T construidas por Kerr Stuart en 1902. Otra linea, el FC de la Mina de la Joya, tenía unos 14,5km de largo, pero el autor no ha podido encontrar información sobre su ancho de vía o de su parque de locomotoras.

A diferencia de las otras lineas de la región, el FC del Guadiana, el cual servía las Minas de Herrerías, quedaba totalmente aislado de la red general de ferrocarriles. Por sus vías de 762mm bajaba el mineral unos 20km hasta las orillas del río Guadiana, que forma la frontera entre España y Portugal aquí. Las primeras locomotoras eran una 0-2-0ST comprada a Black Hawthorn y tres 0-3-0T suministradas por John Fowler, mientras que tres 0-3-0T fueron compradas a St. Leonard durante los años veinte. Pero durante los sesenta la mayoría de los trenes tenían tracción diesel y cuando la linea fue cerrada en 1966 dos de las máquinas Ruhrtaler fueron trasladadas a la linea de San Telmo.

Puerto de la Laja, donde era embarcado el mineral, está a pocos kilómetros de Pomerao, en la orilla portuguesa del Guadiana, donde había otro muelle y desde donde subía otro ferrocarril, de 16km y de 1067mm, hasta unas minas. Igual que el FC del Guadiana, no tenía enlace con la red general de los ferrocarriles portugueses y era de origen inglés. Al principio había tracción de sangre y las primeras locomotoras de vapor, unas 0-2-0WT compradas a Hawthorn (Leith), llegaron en 1864. Luego llegó un surtido de productos de las constructoras inglesas, tales como Hunslet, Kerr Stuart, Kitson y Manning Wardle. En 1926 fue comprada al FC de Río Tinto una 0-4-0T construida por Beyer Peacock. Se dice que una 0-2-0ST, MOSQUITO, era de construcción artesanal de los talleres del ferrocarril en São Domingo en 1922. Tres 0-2-0T construidas por Peckett en 1952 eran las máquinas más modernas de la linea. Poco a poco el río se hizo innavegable, provocando el cierre de la linea a mediados de los sesenta.

Nos desplazamos ahora hacia el este para visitar el FC de las Minas de la Peña de Hierro, de 600mm, cerca de Nerva. Al principio las 0-2-0T construidas por Borsig alrededor de 1900 bajaban el mineral hasta las vías del FC de Río Tinto. No obstante, después de un altercado por las tarifas, Peña Copper Mines Ltd. buscó otra salida firmando un acuerdo con las Minas de Cala para prolongar su linea de vía métrica desde Minas Castillo de las Guardas hasta La Peña (una distancia de 21km). Luego el mineral bajaba hasta los muelles del río Guadalquivir, cerca de Sevilla. Puesto que la concesión era para un ferrocarril público, había trenes de viajeros; en 1921 dos trenes al día enlazaban San Juan de Aznalfarache con Peña de Hierro, un recorrido de 92km. Solo faltaban 11km para formar un enlace físico con las lineas del Río Tinto y de San Juan del Puerto (de un ancho distinto). En teoría era posible durante los años veinte realizar el recorrido entre Sevilla y Huelva por la vía estrecha en un día, aunque con aquel paseo de 11km por la carretera habría sido un día muy largo. El autor no sabe cuando acabó el servicio de viajeros. Dos de las locomotoras de las Minas de La Peña, unas 1-4-0T construidas por Krauss, fueron vendidas más tarde al FC de La Robla (la No. 120) y al FC de Santander a Bilbao (la No. 61).

Seguimos ahora hacia Zafra en la linea de vía ancha procedente de Sevilla y bajamos en Fuente del Arco, desde donde fue posible viajar hasta Puertollano, por Peñarroya, una distancia de 218km por la vía métrica. En su mayor parte, el parque de vapor del FC de Puertollano a Peñarroya era de procedencia francesa con unas 0-3-0T y 0-4-0T construidas por Fives-Lille entre 1894 y 1907, unas 1-3-0T compradas a SACM en 1914, dos 1-4-0T suministradas por La Meuse y tres 1-5-0 construidas en Francia en 1927 y compradas a los ferrocarriles de Túnez en 1953. La única locomotora alemana era una 0-3-3-0T, producto de la casa de Henschel. Casi todas las locomotoras tenían nombres.

En Peñarroya las minas de carbón de ENCAR tenían una red de vía ancha, con trenes de viajeros y empalme con la linea de RENFE, mientras que la fundición de plomo tenía una red de vía métrica que enlazaba con la linea del PP. Era la propiedad de la empresa minera que había construido el PP, y por sus vías circulaban dos 0-3-0T.

Entre Conquista y Puertollano, una distancia de 50km, el PP había sido electrificado con 3000V en 1927 a causa de las fuertes pendientes de este tramo, también contaba con un parque de locomotoras eléctricas francesas. Bajo la gestión de FEVE fueron introducidos algunos automotores para los servicios de viajeros, pero el cierre tuvo lugar en 1970.

La Sociedad Minera y Metalúrgica de Peñarroya (SMMP), que había construido el PP, era de origen francés (de ahí sus locomotoras francesas) y fue fundada en 1881 con su sede en Puertollano. Para su red de vías hulleras de Puertollano tenía un parque de vapor de vía ancha (unas 0-3-0T y 0-5-0T de procedencia francesa o belga), pero también había una máquina de vía métrica, la cual anteriormente había estado en el parque del PP. Además, en Mina Andrubal había una red de 640mm; era propiedad de la SMMP y tenía unas 0-3-0T construidas por Couillet.

Como el lector puede suponer, la cuenca minera de Puertollano era una zona poco atractiva para el turista que no se interesaba por los ferrocarriles industriales. Sin embargo, hacia el este salía una preciosa linea de 750mm, la cual terminaba su recorrido de 76km en la estación de Valdepeñas, en el ferrocarril principal de Madrid a Córdoba y Sevilla. Dejó atrás la industria y penetraba por una región rural donde predomina la viticultura. El parque de vapor consistía en tres 0-3-0 (originalmente 0-3-0T) construidas por Couillet entre 1891 y 1894, dos 0-2-1 suministradas por Jung en 1903 y una 0-3-0 comprada a O & K en 1903. Posteriormente la linea fue incorporada en la EFE, siendo cerrada en 1963.

Al sur de Despeñaperros en la linea de Sevilla el ferrocarril métrico de Linares a La Carolina cerró en 1961. Había sido construido para servir las minas de plomo, pero en 1954 había solamente dos trenes de mercancías cada día; tardaban dos horas en recorrer los 39km, sin duda con muchos retrasos para efectuar maniobras. El parque de vapor consistía en cuatro 0-4-0T construidas por St. Leonard en 1908.

También en Linares había un ferrocarril ligero interurbano con tracción eléctrica, conocido como el FC Eléctrico de La Loma; había sido inaugurado en 1907 y era de vía métrica, con una corriente de 600V. Enlazaba Baeza-Empalme (en la linea de Madrid a Granada) con Ubeda (23km) y Baeza Ciudad (por un ramal de 5km, que partía de La Yedra). En Linares, la red de tranvías urbanos fue inaugurada en 1902 y luego, en 1914, fue acabada una linea de 6,5km entre este pueblo y Baeza-Empalme, con enlace en San Roque con la linea de vía métrica con tracción vapor. A partir de aquella fecha la red entera entre Linares y Ubeda era gestionada como una sola empresa, siendo incorporada en la EFE en 1936. En 1953 empezaron las obras para transformar la red, por entonces bastante deteriorada, en un moderno ferrocarril ligero electrificado con 1500V y con explanación propia. El trabajo siguió hasta principios de los sesenta; algunos tramos fueron inaugurados, muchos terraplenes y trincheras fueron construidos y una nueva terminal fue acabada (pero sin colocar las vías) en 1962. Nuevas unidades fueron suministradas, aunque nunca entraron en servicio. Hacia 1964 las obras se habían paralizado y dos años más tarde el sistema fue cerrado.

Durante la visita del autor a la linea, tuvo lugar un incidente curioso, el cual fue descrito en la revista *Modern Tramway* en 1964; citamos:

'Seguimos la carretera entre Linares, Baeza-Empalme y Tres Olivas sin ver ni un solo tranvía; paramos cerca de La Yedra para sacar fotos. Había un rebaño de cabras en las vías; tendrían que moverse, ya que según el horario, un tranvía pronto iba a llegar ... pero nunca llegó. Cuando nos acercamos a la estación de La Yedra, descubrimos el por qué. El tranvía, que se había descarrilado, estaba rodeado por más de cien Guardias Civiles, por lo visto la cuasa del descarrilamiento fue una sobrecarga de los vehículos antiguos. Los maquinistas, desafiando la ley de entonces, se habían puesto en huelga en señal de protesta. Seguimos hasta Ubeda (el centro de formación de la Guardia Civil), la ciudad estaba abarrotada, ya que había una multitud de guardias esperando bajar en tranvía hasta la estación de RENFE.

77. On 25 May 1962, a Coin train is seen leaving Málaga behind another Tubize 0-6-0T, in much smarter condition. *(L G Marshall)*

78. On shed at Málaga Casa Misericordia depot in 1962 is a very derelict rack tank that will not see service again. *(Author)*

79/80. Two rare views of the rack section beyond Vélez-Málaga; one is dated 1921 but no other details are known. *(Author's collection)*

Anochecía cuando regresamos a Baeza-Empalme. Aquí, la comunidad pequeña que rodeaba la estación de RENFE estaba a tope, ya que dos tranvías llenos de Guardias Civiles acababan de llegar con mucho retraso. Los bares estaban haciendo un negocio fenomenal. Parece que este contingente de guardias recién graduados había perdido su tren (con coches reservados) a Madrid y tuvo que viajar, en cambio, en el expreso de noche, que llegó ya a tope a Baeza-Empalme.'

Otro tranvía que fue incorporado en la EFE fue el de Granada a la Sierra Nevada, de ancho de vía de 750mm. Se inauguró entre Granada y Maitena en 1925; luego se cerró en 1931 y pasó a la EFE, la cual, durante los cincuenta lo prolongó hasta San Juan, a 21km de Granada y a una altura de 1160m. Había otros proyectos para prolongar la linea y para construir unos complejos de deportes invernales, pero nunca fueron llevados a cabo; la linea se cerró en 1974.

Granada también tenía una red de tranvías urbanos e interurbanos de vía métrica. Una de estas lineas (de 30km) acabó en Dúrcal, donde comenzó un largo tranvía aéreo de uso industrial, que alcanzó la costa en Motril. Existía un ferrocarril de vía métrica que enlazaba el pueblo y el puerto de Motril con Puerto de Calahonda (un recorrido de 13km). Hace muchos años puede que hubiera habido un servicio de viajeros, pero en 1962 quedaron solamente tres locomotoras apartadas; una 0-2-0T y una 0-3-0T construidas por O & K y una 0-2-0T construida por Couillet en 1883. Parece que todas pertenecían al Puerto de Motril.

◻ ◻ ◻ ◻ ◻ ◻ ◻ ◻

Así termina la primera parte de nuestro recorrido por la vía estrecha española. En el Tomo 2 comenzaremos en Madrid y nos dirigiremos hacia el noreste, luego siguiendo las lineas de la costa hasta Ferrol, al acabar con lo que era el último bastión de la tracción vapor de España, el FC de Ponferrada a Villablino.

81. The 1.15pm Málaga to Vélez in the suburbs of Málaga on 20 April 1961. The locomotives are 0-6-0T's Nos. 26 (Tubize) and 42 (SLM). No. 42 was not in steam but was being taken to help with track lifting on the closed rack section. *(J Wiseman)*

82/83. Two scenes near Carvajal, on the Fuengirola line, in October 1955. The rugged nature of the landscape makes it difficult to believe that the coastal resort of Torremolinos, then beginning to develop, is only a few miles distant. Today this is a busy broad gauge electrified line!

(Both: J Wiseman)

84. Seville - Minas de Cala: the sad scene of dereliction at the depot on 27 April 1982. On the shed road are No.34 BARRENRA and No.33 GUADALQUIVIR (Borsig). To the right of these 0-4-0T's is a line of Borsig 0-6-4T's, the front one being No.3 ZUFRE of 1904. *(Author)*

85. A broadside look at ZUFRE reveals the size of these machines. *(Author)*

86. Seville - Aznalcóllar: On 5 April 1956 a freight arrives at Camas, the metre gauge locomotive hauling broad gauge wagons.....note the dual gauge track. The locomotive is No.13 POZOBLANCO, an 0-8-0T built by Fives-Lille in 1903 and on loan from the Peñarroya - Puertollano railway.

(Author)

87. On 25 March 1965 Jung built 0-6-2T No.4 GUADIAMAR is in use. *(Author)*

88. On 31 March 1966 the working locomotive at Camas is No.5, a Krauss built 0-6-2T of 1908.
(L G Marshall)

89. A general view taken in 1965. On the left are Nos.3 and 1, while in the depot entrance is No.5.
(Author)

Pages 77/78: the Rio Tinto has been illustrated extensively in another volume. But of some interest is this extract from the "Beyer-Peacock Quarterly Review," published in 1931 and giving prominence to the Company's locomotives supplied to the Railway. (Plateway Press)

As early as 1875 we built twelve tank locomotives of the 0-6-0 wheel arrangement for the Rio Tinto Company. The principal dimensions of these engines were as follows: cylinders, outside, 15" x 20"; the diameter of the wheels 3' 3½"; the rigid wheel base 10' 9"; the working pressure of the boiler 130 lb. per square inch and the total heating surface 659 square feet. The total weight in working order was 26 tons.

A photograph of one of these locomotives is reproduced herewith.

We delivered a further two of this type of engine in 1890.

In 1898 we built three tank locomotives of the 0-8-0 wheel arrangement. These engines weighed, in working order, 40½ tons and had a boiler pressure of 180 lb. per square inch. The cylinders, as will be seen from the accompanying illustration, were outside and had a diameter of 16" x 22" stroke. The heating surface of the boiler was 800.5 sq. ft. and the diameter of the wheels was 3' 6". They had a water-tank capacity of 1,000 gallons and a bunker capacity of 50 cubic feet. A further three of these engines were delivered in 1907.

Many of the early locomotives we built are still in service in the mines.

The two "Beyer-Garratt" locomotives, delivered to the Rio Tinto Company in 1930 for hauling the heavy pyrites and sulphur traffic between the Rio Tinto Mines and the Port of Huelva, work over a line of 52 miles in length of 3' 6" gauge, the first 45 miles from Huelva to Frailes having a maximum gradient of 1 in 100, the ruling grade thereafter being 1 in 50. The total rise in the 52 miles is about

0-6-0 Locomotive for the Rio Tinto Mines Ltd., built by Beyer, Peacock & Co. in 1875.

0-8-0 Locomotive for the Rio Tinto Mines Ltd., built by Beyer, Peacock & Co. in 1898.

April, 1931   The Beyer-Peacock Quarterly Review

Showing outlet of Tunnel No. 5. This tunnel runs through the Mines of South Lode, Alfredo, Guillermo to Atalaya, and is about five miles in length. The village of Naya is also shown with chimneys from the smelter.

Frailes where the train was split and only 250 tons gross load could be taken from Frailes to Rio Tinto.

The rolling stock used for these trains consists of all-steel bogie waggons, equipped with the vacuum brake, and weighing 12 tons. They have a carrying capacity of 30 tons so that the down trains, usually composed of 50 of these waggons, haul 2,000 tons.

1,000 feet. The track is well ballasted and laid with 65 lb. flat bottom rails; considerable curvature exists, the minimum radius being 100 metres.

The engines are giving good service hauling loads of 550 tons over the 1 in 50 grade from Frailes to Rio Tinto. Prior to the introduction of the "Beyer-Garratt" locomotives 40-ton engines were employed, hauling loads of 400 tons up to

These furnaces are used to reduce the Ferric Iron in the Copper Liquors before the precipitation of the copper on pig iron or scrap iron. The liquor treated results from washing the mineral heaps with water and, in addition to the copper which has been extracted from the mineral, it also contains a certain proportion of Ferric Iron which attacks the iron in the cementation tanks. The treated liquor gravitates into a dam and thence is allowed to flow into the tanks, where the copper is precipitated with considerable economy in the consumption of scrap iron or pig.

90. Buitron Railway: No.1 VICTORIA at Valverde, 25 March 1961. *(L G Marshall)*

91. Tharsis Railway: On 23 September 1963 0-4-0T No.1 ODIEL, built by Dübs in 1867, was at Corrales. *(Author)*

92. On line working was 2-8-0T No.39 THARSIS (Hohenzollern 1926) fitted with Giesl ejector, and seen here near Corrales. *(Author)*

93. This was the day of the once-weekly passenger train, a single coach tacked on to the end of a long rake of wagons. It is hauled by No. 38 CHANZA, another Hohenzollern 2-8-0T, this one built in 1923. *(Author)*

94. Société Française de Pyrites: On 27 September 1963 0-6-0T No.6 (Hartmann 1907) was derelict and unlikely to work again. *(Author)*

95. Mason and Barry, Portugal: the locomotives here bore names, but not numbers. The most modern of three 2-6-0T's on the line was this massive example from Kitson in 1932 named JOSE DANINO. It is seen at Pomerão on 24 September 1963. *(Author)*

96. DUORO is one of a trio of Peckett 0-4-0T's supplied in 1952. *(Author)*

97. This area of Portugal must have been very different when BRANGANZA, an 0-4-0WT from Hawthorns of Leith, came here new in 1874. One imagines that it would have been delivered by sea and river to Pomerão. The first of this large batch had been built in 1865 and fifteen had been delivered by 1874, plus some Hunslet 0-6-0T's. *(Author)*

98. Peñarroya - Puertollano:Fives-Lille 0-8-0T No.4 PUERTOLLANO is one of the first batch of locomotives supplied to the railway and in April 1962 was in action at the SMM works, the only metre gauge locomotive used there, although the works had a fleet of broad gauge 0-10-0T's. *(Author)*

99. 2-6-0T No.21 arrives at Peñarroya with a passenger working from Fuente del Arco on 4 April 1961. *(J Wiseman)*

100. The SMM also had a 640mm gauge system at Mina Asdrubal, which connected with the broad gauge. On 23 April 1962 Couillet 0-4-0T No.2 was on shed but a sister engine was working. *(Author)*

101. Back on the metre gauge, on 20 September 1963, 0-6-0T ALMODOVAR DEL CAMPO (Fives-Lille 1894) is in charge of freight wagons being loaded at Peñarroya. *(Author)*

102. The railway had a trio of 4-6-0T's built by SACM(G) in 1914. This one is No.20 PUEBLONUEVO DEL TERRIBLE, with another of the same class behind. This photograph was taken in 1962. *(Author)*

103. Electric No.105 at Puertollano, 29 March 1966. *(J Wiseman)*

104. Valdepeñas - Puertollano: on 22 April 1962 No.6 ASTURIAS (O&K 1903) arrives at Puertollano, very much the industrial end of the line. *(Author)*

105. No.1 VITORIA (Couillet 1891) pauses at Aldea del Rey with the Puertollano - Valdepeñas "correo" on 20 May 1962. *(L G Marshall)*

106. No.6 ASTURIAS is seen again, this time at Valdepeñas with the 7.30am to Puertollano on 20 May 1962.

(*L G Marshall*)

107. In a portrait epitomising the appeal of the Spanish narrow gauge, BELGICA No.3 (Couillet 1894), is seen crossing the train on which I am travelling at Calzada. The date is 22 April 1962. *(Author)*

108. Linares - La Carolina: closed by April 1962, all that is left in the roofless shed is No.4 SAN ROQUE, an 0-8-0T from St. Leonard in 1908. *(Author)*

109. A few years earlier there was activity. No.2 LINARES is seen at San Roque on 12 October 1959. *(J Wiseman)*

110: Linares interurban: the new light railway that never was! Ubeda station in 1962, complete except for the tracks that were never to arrive. *(Author)*

111. The old system was still functioning. Electric loco L22 and passenger trailer at Ubeda depot. *(Author)*

112/113. Two views of the 'Civil Guard' special, described in the text. *(Author)*

114. Sierra Nevada: On 8 April 1956 car no.4 is pictured at Pinos Genil en route from Granada to San Juan. *(Author)*

115. A vintage view of the line, dating from 1941, showing the rugged scenery traversed by the tramway. *(Archivo E Andres Gramage)*

APPENDIX
SPANISH RAILWAYS 1967-68

The following table, extracted from *Jane's World Railways, 1967-68*, gives a list of the Spanish 'common carrier' railways operating at that time, and filing a return. Of the 58 railways (and tramways) listed, no less than 55 are narrow gauge. The statistics make fascinating reading, though caution is needed in interpreting the motive power figures given (col 5): traditionally, 'official' returns give the number of locomotives in capital stock (which might include a number set aside for scrapping), rather than those in service. It is interesting to note even a primarily freight railway like the Buitron a San Juan del Puerto claiming to be carrying 136,700 passengers a year, though the figure claimed for the Río Tinto Railway (1,359,200) cannot be correct, as by this late date passenger services were down to two trains per week, and this would imply 13,000 passengers per train! The true figure is probably closer to that claimed by the Ferrocarril de Tharsis (14,700 per year). Of note also is the residual freight traffic carried by primarily passenger carrying concerns, eg FC de Soller (11,500 tonnes), FC Urola (38,300 tonnes), even the Granada to Sierra Nevada electric tramway managing a praiseworthy 1,400 tonnes! Excluded from this Appendix for reasons of space are average speeds, but top performance for passenger services is claimed by the Ferrocarril del Cantabrico (31 mph), and Ferrocarriles de le Robla (26 mph). Several more, including Ponferrada - Villablino and Olot -Gerona, claim 25 mph averages. At the other end of the scale the FC Tharsis clocks in at a sedate 14 mph, though as theirs were mixed trains, comparisons are perhaps unfair. And anyway, which reader of this book, given the opportunity to travel on many of the long-abandoned railways featured in this survey, would wish to hurry over his journey?

		1	2	3	4	5	6	7	8	9	10	11	12	13	14	
										Freight movement				Passengers		
	NAME OF COMPANY ADDRESS	Gauge ft. in. *(metres)*	Route length incl. **E**=Electrified miles *(km.)*	Track system incl. **E**=Electrified miles *(km.)*	Elect. system and type of conductor	Locomotives L=Line S=Shunt **S**team **E**lectric **D**iesel **De**=elec. **Dh**=hyd.	Rail-cars **E**lectric **D**iesel **T**railer **R**ailbus **M**ultiple **U**nit set	Pass. train cars	Freight train cars **C**ontainers	Total Volume carried Thousands of tonnes	Av'ge haul per ton miles *(km.)*	Av'ge net train load tonnes	Max. trailing load tonnes	Total number carried in. 1000's	Average journey miles *(km.)*	
	SPAIN *(See page 221)*															
9	**Red Nacional de los Ferrocarriles Españoles (R.E.N.F.E.)** Santa Isabel 44, Madrid Dir. Gen.: D. Carlos Roa Rico	5′ 5$\frac{11}{16}$″ *(1·674)*	8,303 *(13,405)* **E** 1,825 *(2,938)*	11,705 *(18,849)* **E** 2,306 *(3,713)*	1,350 V. 1,500 V. &3,000V d.c. 6,000 V. 3/25	**SL** 1739 **SS** 118 **EL** 363 **De**L193 **De**S 225 **Dh**L 15 **Dh**S 21 **DS** 46	**B** 61 **E** 16 **D** 91 **E**m**U** 210 **D**mu 80 **DT** 148 **ET** 286	2,967	60,895 **C** 3,594	31,998·5	182 *(293)*	187·0		156,535·0	50 *(80)*	9
10	**Ferrocarril de las Minas de Aznalcollar al Guadalquiver** Av. Queipo de Llano No. 15, Seville	3′ 3$\frac{3}{8}$″ *(1·00)*	27 *(43)*	30 *(48)*		**S** 6			175	83·9	15·5 *(25)*	260	450			10
11	**Ferrocarril de Alcoy al Puerto de Gandia** S. Francisco do Borja 56, Gandia	3′ 3$\frac{3}{8}$″ *(1·00)*	33 *(53)*			**S** 6		15	177	20·4				219·9		11
12	**Com. F.C. Estratégicos Secundarios de Alicante** Av. Villajoyosa, Alicante	3′ 3$\frac{3}{8}$″ *(1·00)*	60 *(97)*	60 *(97)*		**S** 9	2	38	116	21·9	37 *(60)*			497·2	19 *(30)*	12
13	**Ferrocarril de Astillero a Ontaneda** Santander	3′ 3$\frac{3}{8}$″ *(1·00)*	22 *(35)*			**S** 5	2	12	64	36·1				381·9		13
14	**Ferrocarriles Económicos de Asturias** Avda, Santander, Oviëdo	3′ 3$\frac{3}{8}$″ *(1·00)*	71 *(115)*			**S** 29	**D** 2 **T** 2	46	975	603·7	50 *(80)*	300	430	1,723·1	16·8 *(27)*	14
15	**Ferrocarriles del Bidasoa** Irun	3′ 3$\frac{3}{8}$″ *(1·00)*	32 *(52)*			**S** 7	3	7	58	14·3				116·3		15
16	**Ferrocarriles Y Transportes Surburbanos de Bilbao S.A.** Bilbao	3′ 3$\frac{3}{8}$″ *(1·00)*	**E** 37 *(59)*	**E** 47 *(76)*	1,500 V. d.c. OH	**S** 3	**E** 18 **EMU** 10	50	172	206·9				15,658·0	6·5 *(10·4)*	16
17	**Ferrocarril de Minas de Cala** Bailen 9, Bilbao	3′ 3$\frac{3}{8}$″ *(1·00)*	91 *(146)*													17
		1	2	3	4	5	6	7	8	9	10	11	12	13	14	

	NAME OF COMPANY ADDRESS	1	2	3	4	5	6	7	8	9	10	11	12	13	14	
										Freight movement				Passengers		
		Gauge ft. in. (*metres*)	Route length incl. E=Electrified miles (*km.*)	Track length incl. E=Electrified miles (*km.*)	Elect. system and type of conductor	Locomotives L=Line S=Shunt Steam Electric Diesel De=elec. Dh=hyd.	Railcars Electric Diesel Trailer Railbus Multiple Unit set	Pass. train cars	Freight train cars Containers	Total Volume carried. Thousands of tonnes	Av'ge haul per ton miles (*km.*)	Av'ge net train load tonnes	Max. trailing load tonnes	Total number carried in 1000's	Average journey miles (*km.*)	
	SPAIN (*contd.*)															
1	**Ferrocarril de Olot a Gerona** Aviño 50, Barcelona (*State operated by No. 6/p. 30*)	3' 3⅜" (*1·00*)	34 (*55*)	41 (*65·8*)		SL 9	D 2	25	126							1
2	**F.C. de Ponferrada a Villablino** Alcala 27, Madrid Dir.: D. M. Jorisse y Braecke	3' 3⅜" (*1·00*)	40 (64)	56 (*91*)		SL 22 SS 2		22	352*	2,098·8	29 (*46·6*)	218	650	381·4	21 (*33·8*)	2
3	**F.C. E. de Reus a Salou** Carreterra Salou, Reus	3' 3⅜" (*1·00*)	5 (9)	6 (*10*)		S 4		20		3·9		17		229·9		3
4	**Compañia Española de Minas de Rio Tinto S.A.** Minas de Rio Tinto, Huelva Gen. Man.: Don Antonio de Torres Espinosa	3' 6" (*1,067*)	57 (92)	202 (*325*)		SL 7 SS 80 DhS 1 De 4		50	65	1,105·3	33·4 (*53·8*)	116	2,324	1,359·2	3·4 (*5·5*)	4
5	**Ferrocarriles de la Robla** Bailen 5, Bilbao Gen. Man.: Z. Cosialls	3' 3⅜" (*1·00*)	211 (340)	242 (*390*)		SL 45 DeL 18 D 8		82	1,160	725·7	73 (*117*)	170	900	1,065·3	29 (46)	5
6	**Ferrocarril Secundario de Sadaba a Gallur** Gallur, Zaragozo	3' 3⅜" (*1·00*)	35 (56)			S 5	2	9	96	58·4				118·0		6
7	**Ferrocarril de San Feliu de Guixols a Gerona** San Feliu de Guixols (Gerona) (*State operated by No. 6/p. 30*)	2' 5½" (*0·75*)	25 (*40*)	29 (*46*)		SL 6		21	106				135			7
8	**Ferrocarril de Santander a Bilbao, S.A.** Bailén 2, Bilbao (*Operated by No. 6/p. 30*)	3' 3⅜" (*1·00*)	92 (*147*)	114 (*183*)												8
9	**Sociadad Explotadora de Ferrocarriles y Tranvias (S.E.F.T.)** Peñaflorida 6, San Sebastian	3' 3⅜" (*1·00*)	E 13 (*21*)	E 19 (*31*)	500 V. d.c.	EL 2	E 9	120	36	50·7	4·2 (*6·7*)	36	150	2,944·2	4·3 (*7·0*)	9
10	**Ferrocarril del Tajuna, S.A.** Avenue Menedez Pelayo, 67 Madrid	3' 3⅜" (*1·00*)	32 (*52*)	37 (*60*)		SL 3 DE 5 DS 1	D 1		129	973·0	19·8 (*32*)	200	600			10
11	**Ferrocarriles Secundarios del Sur de España** (*State operated by No. 6/p. 30*)	3' 3⅜" (*1·00*)	84 (*133*)													11
12	**Ferrocarril de Tharsis a Rio Odiel** Cia. de Azufre y Cobre de Tharsis Ltda. Minas de Tharsis, Huelva	4' 0" (*1·219*)	28 (46)	43 (69)		S 30 D 10		8	734	722·1	27 (43)	355		14·7		12
13	**F.C. de Tortosa a La Cava** (*State operated by No. 6/p. 30*)	3' 3⅜" (*1·00*)	17 (27)													13
14	**Urola (Ferrocarril de Zumarraga a Zumaya)** San Sebastian	3' 3⅜" (*1·00*)	E 23 (37)	E 27 (44)	1,600 V. d.c. OH		E† 10	20	108	38·3	14 (22·6)	59	320	898·0	7·2 (*11·6*)	14
15	**Ferrocarril de Utrillas a Zaragoza** Los Madraza 10, Madrid (*State operated by No. 6/p. 30*)	3' 3⅜" (*1·00*)	79 (*127*)			S 21	2	6	293							15
16	**Compañia de Tranvias y Ferrocarriles de Valencia** Calle Orilla del Rio 2, Valencia (*State operated by No. 6/p. 30*)	3' 3⅜" (*1·00*)	E 71 (*114*)	E 99 (*159*)	500 V. d.c. OH	ES 14	E 28	65	508							16
17	**Ferrocarriles Vasco-Asturiana** Jovellanos 17, Ovieda	3' 3⅜" (*1·00*)	65 (*105*)	84 (*135*)		S 38		53	1,633	1,859·7	36 (*57·9*)	117	5,209	2,929·0	10·8 (*17·5*)	17
18	**Ferrocarriles Vascongados** Achuri 8, Bilbao	3' 3⅜" (*1·00*)	E 98 (*158*)	E 105 (*169*)		S 7 E 17	E 18 D 2	136	895	537·1				7,947·1		18
19	**F.C. Electrico de Vigo a La Ramallosa** Tranvias Electricos de Vigo, S.A. Ave. de la Florida 2, Vigo (Pontevedra)	3' 3⅜" (*1·00*)	E 13 (*21*)				E 10	10	10							19
20	**Compañia de los Ferrocarriles Economicas de Villena a Alcoy y Yecla** Avenido de José Antonio 51, Madrid (*State operated by No. 6/p. 30*)	3' 3⅜" (*1·00*)	85 *136*			S 9		48	184							20
21	**Ferrocarril de Soller, S.A.** Castaner 7, Soller, Majorca A=Palma Section B=Puerto de Soller Section	3' 0" (*0·914*)	E 20 (32)	E 22 (35)	1,200 V. d.c. OH	E 4	E 6 T 7	A 10 B 7	36	11·5	16·3 (26·2)	2·8	120	A.492·8 B.863·4	A. 15·5 (*24·1*) B. 2·7 (4·4)	21
1	**Ferrocarril del Cantabrico** Plaza de las Estaciones, Santander	3' 3⅜" (*1·00*)	65 (*105*)	88 (*141*)		S 26 D 1	D 2 T 3	56	818	880·8	32·3 (52)	260	300	1,852·5	13·7 (22)	1
2	**Ferrocarril de Carreño** Marques de San Estaban 2, Gijon	3' 3⅜" (*1·00*)	E 12 (20)	14 (23)	650 V. d.c.	D 1	E 9 T 14	7	56	172·9	5·7 (9·2)	24	127	4,001·3	6·8 (*11*)	2
3	**Compañia de F.C. de Castilla y Ferrocarriles Secundarios** Palencia Palencia (*State operated by No. 6*)	3' 3⅜" (*1·00*)	142 (230)			S 15	D 2	38	219							3
4	**Cia. Gen. de Ferrocarriles Catalanes S.A.** Calle de la Diputacion 239–3, Barcelona Gen. Man.: Don Gonzalo Turrel Moragas	3' 3⅜" (*1·00*)	89 (*143*) E 13 (*21*)	117 (*188*) E 18 (29)	1,500 V. d.c. OH	SL 19 SS 4 EL 4 DL 4 DS 5	E 5 ET 5	80	864	791·7	40 (65)	200	600	8,821·1	7·9 (*12·7*)	4

	NAME OF COMPANY ADDRESS	1 Gauge ft. in. (metres)	2 Route length incl. E=Electrified miles (km.)	3 Track length incl. E=Electrified miles (km.)	4 Elect. system and type of conductor	5 Locomotives L=Line S=Shunt Steam Electric Diesel De=elec. Dh=hyd.	6 Railcars Electric Diesel Trailer Railbus Multiple Unit set	7 Pass. train cars	8 Freight train cars Containers	9 Freight movement Total Volume carried Thousands of tonnes	10 Av'ge haul per ton miles (km.)	11 Av'ge net train load tonnes	12 Max. trailing load tonnes	13 Passengers Total number carried in 1000's	14 Average journey miles (km.)	
	SPAIN *(contd.)*															
5	**Ferrocarriles de Cataluña S.A.** Plaza de Cataluña No. 1, Barcelona Gen. Man.: Don. R. Hernando Frances	4' 8½" *(1·435)*	**E** 25 *(40)*	**E** 27 *(43)*	1,300 V. d.c. OH		**E** 58 **T** 12	64	1					13,689·5	7·4 *(12·0)*	5
6	**Explotacion de Ferrocarriles por El Estado** Agustin de Bethencourt 4, Madrid *Operates 28 State-owned narrow-gauge lines. See Nos. 6/p. 30; 1, 7, 8, 11, 13, 15, 16, 20/p, 32; and:—*															6
7	**Amorebieta-Guernica-Bermeo** Guernica (Vizcayo)	3' 3⅜" *(1·00)*	15 (25)	17 (27)		**S** 7		15	45	13·2	10 *(17)*			833·8	*(11·3)*	7
8	**Buitrón a San Juan del Puerto** Valverde de Camino (Huelva)	3' 6" *(1·067)*	48 (78)	52 (83)		**S** 14	**D** 1	10	235	41·1	*(52·4)*			136·7	*(18·4)*	8
9	**Calahorra a Arnedillo** Calahorra (Logroño)	3' 3⅜" *(1·00)*	22 (36)	24 (39)		**S** 5	3†	19	60	13·2	*(28·1)*			162·5	*(14·6)*	9
10	**Carcagente a Denia** Valencia	3' 3⅜" *(1·00)*	41 (66)	46 (74)		**S** 14	2†	21	254	22·9	*(58·7)*			384·9	(22)	10
11	**Cartagena-la Union los Blancos** Cartagena (Murcia)	3' 5¾" *(1·06)*	10 *(16)*	17 (28)		**S** 7		22	323	73·1	*(9·1)*			441·8	(7·4)	11
12	**Castro-Urdiales-Traslaviña** Castro Urdiales	3' 3⅜" *(1·00)*	21 (33)	24 (39)		**S** 8		4	86	45·0	*(17·9)*			161·6	(8·8)	12
13	**Granada a Sierra Nevada** Granada	2' 5½" *(0·75)*	**E** 13 *(21)*		1,200 V. d.c. OH		**E** 4 **T** 6		14	1·4	*(11·3)*			160·7	(9·7)	13
14	**Ferrocarril Electrico de La Loma** Linares (Jaén)	3' 3⅜" *(1·00)*	**E** 17 (27)	**E** 19 *(31)*	6,000 V. d.c. OH	**E** 2	**E** 21		24	14·8	(22)			287·8	*(15·1)*	14
15	**Tranvias de Linares** Linares	3' 3⅜" *(1·00)*	**E** 12 *(19)*	**E** 13 (20)	600 V. d.c. OH	All stock included in F. C. La Loma				4·4	*(8·8)*			558·7	(6·7)	15
16	**Madrid a Almorox** Madrid	3' 3⅜" *(1·00)*	45 (73)	48 (78)		**S** 11		30	93	7·6	(55)			457·1	(17·2)	16
17	**Málaga (San Juan) a Fuengirola** Málaga	3' 3⅜" *(1·00)*	13 *(21)*			**S** 5	**D** 3	13	19					269·9	(17·7)	17
18	**F.C. de Mallorca** Palma de Mallorca	3' 0" *(0·914)*	132 *(212)*			**S** 16	**D** 6	56	493	84·1	20·5 *(33·1)*			1,036·9	18·6 (30)	18
19	**Manresa a Olván** Barcelona	3' 3⅜" *(1·00)*	31 (50)	32 (52)		**S** 13 **D** 3	**D** 3		178	791·0	(16)			305·1	*(17·8)*	19
20	**F.C. Ferrol-Gijon**	3' 3⅜" *(1·00)*	84 *(136)*													20
21	**Peñarroya-Puertollano** Peñarroya	3' 3⅜" *(1·00)*	150 *(242)* **E** 34 *(55)*	165 *(265)* **E** 37 *(59)*	3,000 V. d.c. OH	**S** 20 **E** 5	**D** 4	34	548	345·2	*(67·5)*			336·2	*(31·5)*	21
22	**F.C. Suburbano de Madrid**	4' 8½" *(1·435)*	**E** 6 *(10)*													22
23	**Vasco-Navarro** Vitoria	3' 3⅜" *(1·00)*	**E** 86 *(139)*	**E** 101 *(163)*	1,200 V. d.c. OH	**S** 3 **D** 1	**E** 16	47	343	187·8	*(20·3)*			1,293·7	*(17·5)*	23
24	**Ferrocarril Secundario de Guardiola a Castellar d'en Huch** Corcega 325, Barcelona	1' 11⅝" *(0·60)*	8 *(12)*	10 *(16)*		**S** 6		6	39	68·0	5 (8)	14	140	10·7	6 (9)	24
25	**Ferrocarril Secundario de Haroa a Ezcaray** Haro (Logrono)	3' 3⅜" *(1·00)*	21 *(34*			**S** 3		13	61							25
26	**Ferrocarril de Langreo en Asturias** Av. Menendez Pelayo 67, Madrid	4' 8½" *(1·435)*	40 (64)	43 *(70)*		**S** 32		36	2,024	2,841·7				2,630·6		26
27	**F.C. Estragetico de Leon a Matallana** *(Operated by F.C. de la Robla).*															27
28	**Ferrocarriles Suburbanos de Málaga** Plaza de Queipo de Llana 1, Malaga	3' 3⅜" *(1·00)*	65 *(105)*	80 *(130)*		**S** 11	**R** 3 **T** 3	25	182	156·2	6·4 *(10·3)*	13·9	160	539·6	10·6 *(17·0)*	28
29	**F.C. de Montaña a Grandes Pendientes** Paseo de Gracia 36, Barcelona 6 *Routes:* Ribas-Caralps-Nuria (Rack) Montserrat-San Juan (Funicular) Montserrat-San Cueva (Funicular)	3' 3⅜" *(1·00)*	**E** 8 *(13)*		1,500 V. d.c. OH	**E** 4		150	12	0·8	*(12)*			175·8	8 *(12)*	29
		1	2	3	4	5	6	7	8	9	10	11	12	13	14	

† Nos. 9 and 10. Petrol (gas).
* Nos. 20 and 22. are new construction.

THE NARROW GAUGE RAILWAYS OF SPAIN
PART 2: CASTILE TO THE BISCAY COAST

continues the story of Spain's narrow gauge railways. This part of the journey starts on the tablelands of central Spain, heads north through Valladolid and Burgos, south east to Zaragoza, then north again to touch the French frontier at Irun, finally exploring the thriving narrow gauge strongholds of Cantabria and Asturias. Railways featured include:-

Madrid suburban (ESTADO)	Cuatro Vientos military railway
FC de Madrid a Aragon	Poveda sugar
Villalba - Berrocal	FC Elecrico del Guadarrama
Castilian Secondary Railways	Haro - Ezcaray
Calahora - Arnedillo	Tudela - Tarazona
Gallur - Sabeda	FC de Cariena a Zaragoza
Zaragoza - Utrillas	Pamplona - Aoiz-Sanguesa
Sociedad Minera Guipuzcoana	SEFT, Irun
Irun - Elizondo	FC Vascongados
Zumaya - Zumarraga	Vasco - Navarro
Guernica - Amorebieta	Sestao - Galdames
AHV Steelworks, Bilbao	Basconia steelworks, Bilbao
FTS Bilbao	Santander - Bilbao
FC La Robla	Hulleras de Sabero, Cistierna
Astillera - Onteneda	Orconera Iron Ore Co., Astillero
Nueva Montana, Santander	FC Cantabrico
Real Compania Asturiana de Minas	Solvay, Torrelavego
FC Economicas de Asturias	Covadonga Steam Tramway
Laviana - Rioseco	SMDF, Santa Anna
FC Carreno	Ribadeo - Villaodrid
Vasco - Asturiana	ENSIDESA, Mieres
Hulleras de Turon	Minas de Aller, Ujo
FC Ponferrada - Villablino	Antracitas de Gaiztarra

This volume is illustrated with maps and approximately 120 black and white photographs. It also contains a Bibliography of works in English and Spanish.

PUBLICATION: April 1995; For full information write to Plateway Press, PO Box 973, Brighton, BN2 2TG, England

LOS FERROCARRILES DE VIA ESTRECHA EN ESPAÑA
PARTE 2: DESDE CASTILLA A LA COSTA CANTABRICA

La segunda parte de este libro, esta prevista para Abril de 1995 y comprende un recorrido desde Madrid por la Meseta Central hacia Valladolid y Burgos; por el sud-este hasta Zaragoza incluyendo el FC de Utrillas; por el Norte desde Irún en el limite de la frontera Francesca y recorriendo la costa Cantabrica, Asturias y acabando finalmente en Galicia.

Este volúmen está totalmente ilustrado con mapas y aproximadamente 120 fotos en blanco y negro.

Texto en Inglés y Español, con una detallada bibliografia de ostros libros y revistas en ambas lenguas sobre la via estrecha en España.

Para información sobre estas publicaciones así como el fondo editorial de Plateway Press dirigirse a: Librimport, Provenza, 277, 08037 BARCELONA, Tel 215 67 96